THE UNMAKING OF A DANCER— AN EXTRAORDINARY TRUE STORY

"I COULDN'T PUT IT DOWN....Ms. Brady's writing is like the best dancing: clean image, strong line, all exquisitely balanced on enchanted air."

—Shana Alexander

"MESMERIZING READING ALL THE WAY...raw, funny, surely crafted storytelling...SUPERB"

—Kirkus Reviews

"A STRONG AND MOVING BOOK...BEAUTIFULLY WRITTEN, DEVASTATINGLY HONEST"

—Harold C. Schonberg,
Dance Critic for *The New York Times*

"Joan Brady...has described the world of the ballet studio and dressing room vividly...(she) captures the smells and chatter and roller-coaster emotions of the dancer's life in all their intensity."

—*The New York Times Book Review*

THE UNMAKING OF A DANCER

An Unconventional Life

Joan Brady

WASHINGTON SQUARE PRESS
PUBLISHED BY POCKET BOOKS NEW YORK

A Washington Square Press Publication of
POCKET BOOKS, a Simon & Schuster division of
GULF & WESTERN CORPORATION
1230 Avenue of the Americas, New York, N.Y. 10020

Published by arrangement with Harper & Row, Publishers Inc.
Library of Congress Catalog Card Number: 81-48030

ISBN: 0-671-46817-0

First Washington Square Press printing March, 1983

10 9 8 7 6 5 4 3 2 1

WASHINGTON SQUARE PRESS, WSP and colophon are
registered trademarks of Simon & Schuster.

Printed in the U.S.A.

Grateful acknowledgment is made for permission to reprint the quotations on page 9.

Quotation from *We* by Eugene Zamiatin, translated by Gregory Zilboorg, copyright 1924 by E. P. Dutton & Co., Inc., renewed 1952 by Gregory Zilboorg. Reprinted by permission of Elsevier-Dutton Publishing Co., Inc.

Excerpt from *Remembrance of Things Past* by Marcel Proust, translated by C. K. Scott Moncrieff, copyright 1934 and renewed 1962 by Random House, Inc. Reprinted by permission of Random House, Inc.

for DWM
in celebration

Why is dance beautiful? Answer:
because it is an *unfree* movement.
Because the deep meaning of the
dance is contained in its absolute,
ecstatic submission, in the ideal
of *non-freedom*.

—Eugene Zamiatin, *We*

We have not managed to surmount the
obstacle, as we were absolutely
determined to do, but life has
taken us round it, led us past it. . . .

—Marcel Proust,
The Sweet Cheat Gone

Ah, love, let us be true
To one another! . . .

—Matthew Arnold, "Dover Beach"

PART I

This is a true story. However, with the exception of my family and certain prominent individuals, I have changed the names of and details about persons described in the book to protect their identities.

A ballet class always opens at the barre with *pliés*. *Pliés* are deep knee bends, done within the confines of ballet's rigid esthetic, but in principle not at all unlike the squat jumps football players perform just before the game begins.

UNTIL I WAS ALMOST TWELVE, the only child in our neighborhood who took ballet lessons was Susan; her backyard and ours were separated by a wooden fence. I was supposed to be learning the piano. Susan's father could whistle scales through his hands; he cupped his stubby fingers over his mouth, puffed out his cheeks, and the notes came out like ascending raspberries. I used to go home, not as sure as I had been that the piano was as awful as it seemed. My mother said Susan's father didn't know anything about *real* music. He played the saxophone on the *Breakfast Club*, a radio program broadcast each morning in San Francisco at six-thirty; that sort of music, my mother said—well, it wasn't *real* music at all.

He was a sandy-haired man, prematurely bald, with round, pink cheeks; in the afternoons, when we got home from school, he used to feed spools into the player piano that stood in Susan's living room, and she and I danced to that while he pumped the pedals. It seemed to me a wonderful thing to have a piano that played itself all by itself, but my mother said it wasn't a *real* piano. On Tuesdays and Saturdays he drove Susan to her ballet lessons; I went along once or twice.

The girls in her class wore fluffy white skirts, as I remember it; doubtless they were practicing for some sort of recital. I took an immediate fancy to the shoes they had on; I could stand on my hands better than anyone in the neighborhood—Susan included—and I bet myself, watching those girls, that I could stand on my toes pretty well too. Besides, ballet lessons looked like fun, and whatever else piano lessons were, they weren't that. Music—*real* music, that is—was a touchy subject in our house at best. When Beethoven boomed out from the record player, my sister Judy and I knew our father was depressed; he sat silent and brooding at the dinner table, and God help us if we upset our milk. Sometimes he was depressed for days; sometimes, especially if the *Archduke* Trio played during the afternoon, he had to have his Spam and baked potato delivered to the door of his study on a tray. When he was angry, Stravinsky took over from Beethoven; when he had a headache, Mahler. Our piano teacher was his best friend.

Our piano teacher was an elegant Irishman, a graduate of Stanford's music school, who had found out the hard way that being Stanford's prize pianist cut little ice in New York; he trembled and twisted his hands when he went to concerts. He didn't have as much money as we did. My mother and father were bringing us up by what they called the Open Door Policy, which meant that we saw them without their clothes on, listened to their frequent fights and heard a selection of adult sorrows—not excluding the tightness of Patrick McKuan's budget. We had the vague notion, Judy and I, that we stood between him and starvation.

Judy did well. Patrick wrote "Good" and "Excellent" at the top of her music sheets and pasted silver and gold stars there. My lessons started some months after hers, and when I got back home from the first one, my father was playing Stravinsky at full volume. He shouted over the heavy percussion—and half in time to it—that I was to go upstairs and sit down at the goddamned piano and practice a whole goddamned hour and be goddamned glad of it. He'd never had a chance like that. There'd been no goddamned piano in his house. He'd been too poor. And I ought to be goddamned grateful. In the year that followed, there were lectures, pleadings, scoldings, but the only time I could work up any interest in the piano at all was when Susan's father whistled scales of raspberries through his cupped hands.

One day when Susan got home from school, she found her father dead on his bed; the newspaper said an empty bottle of barbiturates stood on the table beside him. It also said he'd been discovered by his daughter, "Susanne." Susan was angry that they'd misspelled her name, and she said there were red pills scattered on the carpet and a water glass broken to pieces. She said her father's face was blue and his eyes were rolled back white; there was stuff coming out of his mouth, she said, and she'd gone screaming from the room.

From then on I hid as best I could on Saturday mornings from nine onward, the hour appointed for my piano lesson. I wasn't a very successful hider, though, and when Patrick finally asked me, as I thumped dispiritedly at the keys of the old brown piano in his studio, why I bothered to come at all, I said, "Because Daddy says you need the money."

I didn't have to go back after that, but when I told my parents I wanted to take ballet lessons instead, my father said no. My mother, eyebrow lifted, said that if I continued to ask for them for two years, then perhaps—just perhaps—I might be able to take some. That would have been that, I'm sure, if I'd had strong feet. But like so many others who end up in dance, I didn't. I'd started wearing corrective shoes the year before, and corrective shoes are expensive; when my mother complained to the doctor who'd prescribed them, he suggested a few dancing lessons instead. So it was that my mother took me to Miss Wanda Wenninger's ballet school in nearby Albany; Miss Wanda charged only seven dollars a month for two lessons a week; I could get to her easily on the bus; and ballet was, after all, as my mother said with a sigh, a cultural activity of sorts.

Wanda Wenninger had pendulous lips, bulbous cheeks and protruding eyes, like a gargoyle on a French cathedral; her reddish-blond hair waved thickly and tightly over her head, and she pulled it into a massed net of curls at the nape of her neck. Demonstrating to her class of gangly little girls in shorts and socks and ponytails, she placed one hand on the barre, buried the other somewhere in the folds of bright cloth beneath her enormous bosom, and told us to express ourselves all the way from our diaphragms. Her legs were surprisingly delicate; when she posed in front of the mirror, she lifted her flowing circular skirt to expose, ever so daintily, one dimpled knee, and it was always a matter of wonder to me that such a thing could disappear into such a skirt to marry up in some devious way with the matronly figure that emerged from the waistband.

She wore rings and loose bracelets, necklaces, brooches and earrings, and all of them glinted in the sunlight and jangled when she moved. With one pretty leg raised to forty-five degrees in front of her, she used to tilt her head a little, while a small, artificially sweet smile inveigled its way into the heavy contours of her face; she always studied it—the smile, that is— sometimes adjusting her eyebrows a fraction farther upward, sometimes pulling her large lips fractionally farther away from her teeth, before turning to address her pupils. "I was a pupil of Muriel Stuart's, you know, dear," she would say. "And ballet, dear," she often said, "is a good activity for growing girls. The arts mature one."

"You must admit you've brought her up well, Mildred," the dinner guest said. "There aren't many kids who'd sit so quietly while a tableful of adults talk."

My mother smiled, reaching across to pat me on the shoulder. "Well, she is a little more grown up than most. That's just the way she is."

"Come on now, Mildred," the dinner guest said archly. "Don't be modest."

"I take ballet lessons twice a week." My voice squeaked and I nodded my head two or three times to emphasize the importance of the words.

My mother laughed. "Well, yes, you do—but what . . . ?"

"The arts mature one, Mother."

I was a pupil of Miss Wanda's for about eighteen months; I adored her, enjoyed my lessons, and fairly quickly established myself as the fourth-best dancer in the school—after Miranda and Beverly and a girl with red hair like Miss Wanda's own. I took to toe shoes every bit as easily as I had hoped; I liked jumping about to the thin quaver of Miss Wanda's soprano— we had no music—and I liked expressing myself all the way from my diaphragm. At home I improvised dances to records, and my mother was pleased. My father made it plain that he found the dancing dull but thought I looked charming while I did it. I performed as a little Dutch boy, the partner of Miranda's little Dutch girl, for the Easter meeting of Miss Wanda's ladies' club. My mother got me a pair of black toe shoes (just like Miranda's) when she was in New York, and Miss Wanda choreographed a piece for me to a Chopin Prelude; I performed it for some of my father's students, who were very polite. And I became, at last, Miranda's friend.

Miranda was a year younger than I was, pretty if plump, dark-eyed, blond and, I thought, marvelously gifted. Miss Wanda said so. "Miranda's so expressive," she said. Miranda's parents were strict; her father didn't approve of dancing because it showed too much of a girl's body, but Miranda wanted to be a dancer more than anything else in the world, and I, the loyal friend, decided I wanted to be a dancer more than anything else in the world too. We talked about it often. Miss Wanda's school held no summer session, and Miranda and I made an elegant dollhouse to keep ourselves occupied while we planned our futures as ballerinas; we papered the miniature walls with wallpaper samples given us by a local store and we made furniture from papier-mâché and match sticks. We talked about poems too. Miranda could recite "How do I love thee? Let me count the ways," and I could get through a couple of verses of "The Highwayman."

Miranda's father didn't think little girls should know poems like that; he decided we shouldn't see each other anymore. I spent the rest of that summer more or less alone, brooding about being a dancer. I stroked the satin surface of my black toe shoes as though I were Aladdin with his lamp and posed in front of my bedroom mirror, leg raised to forty-five degrees in front of me, head tilted, face fixed in the lines of Miss Wanda's sweet, artificial smile.

That fall I went to the Anna Head School for Girls; I was doing badly in the public school system, and my father said education was the most important thing there was in a child's life. He taught economics at the University of California at Berkeley. He'd worked his way through college and graduate school—lumberjack, forest ranger, shipyard worker—and he'd had to fight his way through the public school system first, walking three miles from home and back, doing his homework by candlelight, getting up at four in the morning to take the cows out to pasture. He'd had to wear his father's cast-off clothes to school; the kids called him "baggy-pants Brady" until he was more than sixteen, but at the end of it he'd entered Reed College and escaped his father's poverty and religious fanaticism. He also put his younger brother through medical school, and he wasn't going to do less for his own kids, despite the fact that Berkeley was punishing him financially for the stand he'd taken, almost alone with his friend Max Radin, against the loyalty oath the university was pressing on its faculty then.

"Well," said Max, a fat man with a mustache and a wet kiss for Judy and me, "I've thought of a motto to put over Berkeley's new faculty building. You remember *The Wind in the Willows*? Remember when Mole spends that whole night wandering around in the forest pursued by the dark and its beasts? And the next day, at dawn, the rabbits all come out of their holes and Otter gets hold of one and learns that they knew about the fix Mole was in. 'So why didn't any of you *do* something?' Otter asks. 'You could have helped.' 'What, *us*?' said the rabbit. '*Do* something? Us rabbits?' Now, that's what belongs over the new faculty building door. 'What, *us*? *Do* something? Us rabbits?'"

My father laughed, but the hurt of Berkeley's scourging never healed; he never got to be chairman of the department, although he served under some of his own students, and the trustees never let him march in the front lines of the faculty parade in black gown and mortarboard.

During my first term at Anna Head's—I was thirteen and a freshman—my teachers said I hadn't settled down yet. I was doing as poorly there as I had in the public school, and it was only toward the end of the second term that any improvement took place. It had nothing to do with settling down, though, and everything to do with Suki Schorer, who entered as a freshman too, halfway through the first term.

There had been rumors about her for weeks. Her

father was an eminent critic, Mark Schorer, who taught English at Berkeley. He'd been on sabbatical in Italy. He was famous, the kids said; Suki could speak Italian, they said, and she was a ballet dancer. I was somewhat piqued. I was a ballet dancer, as I saw it; it was just that I hadn't blabbed it all around. And I was studying with Miss Wanda Wenninger, who was a pupil of Muriel Stuart's. I did not welcome Suki's appearance in the school.

She was tiny. At that time she hadn't reached her full height, which, when she did, barely touched five feet one, and she was very fragile-looking. The school uniform, worn by girls from the seventh grade upward, wasn't made in sizes small enough for her; gray sweater and starched regulation blouse hung like deflated tissue balloons from her shoulders, emphasizing the strong outward thrust of her breastless rib cage and the imperial straightness of her back. She wore her blond hair in an uncompromising bun, pulled starkly away from a face that belonged on a Victorian doll: heart-shaped, small-mouthed, thin-lipped, large-eyed, round-cheeked. Her skin was almost transparently pale; through it you could see, if you looked closely, the slightest movement of her pulse among the network of blue veins at her temples.

She walked with a strange splayfooted walk, which, because she executed it with complete authority, distinguished her instead of making her ridiculous, and she had none of that timidness common to children entering a strange school for the first time in the middle of a term. She seemed, in fact, as indifferent to her classmates as she was to her badly fitting clothes, and this indifference gave her an air of command no one of the rest of us had ever seen before in someone our own age. She was plainly a most remarkable person.

I was some five inches taller than she and very, very thin; I felt like a clumsy giant next to her then, and the feeling stayed with me as long as I knew her. Her interest in me was, or so it seemed, quite impersonal. She asked me a few questions and looked me over a bit.

"Let's see your legs. Um. A little weak. Nicely shaped, though. Very pretty, in fact. Point your toe. No, not like that. You're sickling. Like this. Um. Good arch. Good body too. Nice and thin. You should stand up straight, you know. Who'd you say you were studying with? Wanda Wenninger? Oh, my God. She's disastrous. A pupil of Muriel Stuart's? You don't say. Well, if she was, Muriel Stuart's a lousy teacher or she was a lousy pupil. Do you know who Muriel Stuart is, anyway? No? Well, then, what's so great about studying with a pupil of hers?"

As it turned out, Suki herself had studied with Miss Wanda for a short time before switching to the San Francisco Ballet School. I'd never heard of the San Francisco Ballet School, and Suki smiled wryly. "Well, you should have. It's the only good school in this half of the country. As a matter of fact, you ought to go there. It looks to me like you've got talent, even though you're pretty old. I could probably get you into Basic 4, though. You'll never learn anything anywhere else around here. You can come and watch a class if you want to."

Suki's mother drove us to San Francisco. On the way, Suki ate a cold and very rare hamburger patty; when she'd finished it, she dipped her fingers in the red juice left in the foil and sucked at them. She was on a protein diet, she told me; she had four more pounds to lose. People in Italy ate too much.

At the time, the San Francisco Ballet shared its studios with a fencing club; swords in scabbards and pictures of fencers hung from the walls. The barre, cantilevered out to make room for the foils behind, ran around all sides of the huge room Suki led me to. Girls with their hair tied back in tight buns stood at regular intervals along it, feet in first position, athletic bodies sternly erect, faces as serious as those of Bemelmans's Madeline and her schoolmates; there were a few boys

too, with groin lumps like wadded-up diapers and muscles etched on nylon-sheathed legs as though in medical
relief. A full wall of mirrors reflected them all back upon
themselves, row upon row of them, physically powerful,
decorous, attentive, intensely quiet. At one end of the
room stood a grand piano, top raised, strings exposed;
behind it sat an elderly, cloche-hatted lady with open-
fingered gloves in black lace.

The teacher, who turned out to be Harold Christensen, was dressed all in tan—tan shirt, tan pants, soft tan
shoes. He took a theatrically deep breath, settled his belt
into place to show how well pulled in his thin belly was,
told his pupils to execute four *pliés* in first position, four
in second, four in fourth, and four in fifth, demonstrating
the movement and the positions as he spoke them, and
left the barre. Across the room from me, Suki wore a
blue leotard and pink tights; I sat in my gray uniform on
a bench to one side. The pianist played an opening chord
and the class began.

2

Tendus battements follow *pliés* at the barre; the slow, steady movement of the exercise strengthens the quadriceps, that large mass of muscle on the front of the thigh, and—as all barre work does—forces the development of ballet's basic distortion, the turn-out.

MIRANDA WASN'T IMPRESSED with my report. "Miss Wanda says they turn you into machines there," she said.

"But you didn't see it. *I* did."

"I bet they didn't express themselves, did they? Miss Wanda says they couldn't express themselves to save their lives."

"I don't know. But they can *do* things. All of them. And there were boys too. And they sweated and strained and they all wore leotards and tights and their hair pulled back, and there was a pianist—"

"That sounds nice. I wish Miss Wanda had a pianist. It always seemed to me—"

"—and the teacher was a man!"

"You're kidding."

"No, and he—"

"Well, I bet he didn't study under Muriel Stuart."

"I don't even know who Muriel Stuart is. And anyhow—"

"She teaches in New York. For George Balanchine. That's where I'm going to go. Miss Wanda says Muriel Stuart will love my dancing—she's very expressive. Besides, people who go to the San Francisco Ballet School never make it in New York."

"How do you know?"

"Miss Wanda told me. They like expressive dancers in New York, she says, and—"

"The San Francisco school has a company of its own. A real company. I wouldn't even have to go to New York."

"Oh, Joan, they'll ruin you. You'll never *really* dance. Miss Wanda says so. What does your mother say?"

I sighed. "No. Just no. She won't even discuss it."

"What does your mother know about it?" Suki asked.

"Only what I told her."

"You mean she's never heard of the company, either? Oh, well, that's different. Have you got tights and a leotard?"

"Yes, but there's no point. She won't—"

"How much do you want to bet? You want to go, don't you? Well, then, don't be silly. You'll be taking class within two weeks. I'll get my father to phone."

My mother was angry. "Look, Joanie," she said, "it's devious. I don't like that. I told you no, and I meant no."

"Oh, come on, Mildred." It was a Saturday, and my father had been working in the yard. His hands were dirty and he held them out in front of him as he spoke. "It's not her fault."

"Of course it is. She got that little Suki and they arranged it together."

"I didn't!"

"Well, what if she did? She plainly couldn't get you to listen to her all on her own."

"So she goes behind my back. And to Mark Schorer, for Christ's sake."

"Where else was there for her to go?"

"Look, Bob, I talked to Miss Wenninger this morning. She says it's a terrible school; and it's terribly expensive. We simply can't afford it, no matter how—"

"And what makes you say that, pray?" My father looked down at the dirt on his hands. "If Mark Schorer can afford it, we can afford it. Are you saying we can't educate our child as well as Mark Schorer can educate his? Is that what you're saying?"

Within a week I purchased, under Suki's direction, a ten-passage ticket on the Berkeley-San Francisco train; under her tutelage, I took the train, then the bus, then the cable car up over the hump in California Street, and entered the doors of the San Francisco Ballet School to register as a student. Suki stood beside me.

"How long have you been studying?" the secretary asked me.

"Almost two years."

"Basic 2," she said. "Name?"

"No, no, no," Suki interrupted. "She's as good as Greta already. She could easily do Basic 4."

"O.K., if you say so." The secretary seemed bored. "Basic 4. Name?" I watched her write my name on a white card. "Show her around, will you, Suki?"

I pulled my hair into a severe bun according to Suki's directions; I wore tights and a leotard—both black—and I stood at the barre in the very room I'd seen for the first time no more than a week before. I put my feet in first position and held my back as straight as I could make it. Without my glasses I couldn't see well enough to pick out my figure from the others reflected in the wall of mirrors across from me, but I could see girls there, several all in black, and I knew I was one of them.

During my initial year at the San Francisco Ballet

School I became privy to many secrets; the most important of them was the secret of toe shoes. What I had learned from Miss Wanda was as nothing; Suki was my tutor, and I listened to no one else.

The toe shoe is an altogether peculiar invention; nobody knows just who conceived it or just when it was originally worn or just why anybody would want to wear such a thing. The literature shows that a relative of the modern variety was in use early enough for the great ballerina Taglioni to comment, rather cattily, in 1820 that her competitors' attempts to dance on their toes led to faulty arm movements. In 1832, however, Taglioni herself appeared on pointe in her father's ballet *La Sylphide*. The idea given out was that dancing on the very tips of the toes gave an ethereal look, an illusion of lightness, a graceful new line. More important at the time, I'm sure, was the simple novelty of the technique; contemporary dancers and choreographers had for many years been trying to complete the extraction of ballet from its position as dogsbody to the other theatrical arts, to give it a character different enough and interesting enough to fill a hall reliably on its own. Raised skirts, exposed ankles, and ladies actually on their toes must have sounded a promising combination. On a more personal level, Taglioni's most noteworthy accomplishment as a dancer was her elevation, her ability to jump, an area of ballet where men are always more impressive than women; it's hard not to suspect that her father figured—and correctly too—that by putting his daughter on pointe he would assure her supremacy over her male rivals, who were unable to master the technique without looking ridiculous.

Whatever the motivations for its development, there's no doubting the mystical importance of the toe shoe to such as I was. There is a coming of age in first squeezing the feet into tiny satin shoes with soft sides and stiffened toe pieces, a confirmation of sorts; even the pain they cause, which can be awful, takes on a mystical significance of its own, like the first blood drawn in battle.

Suki took me to the Capezio store in San Francisco, up several flights in a building on Market Street. It was run by a woman with long red fingernails and an oozing Hollywood manner that turned sharp if she suspected her client wasn't among the gifted ones. Suki, like some latter-day Charon, assured my passage. "Don't bother with the kind you wore at Wanda's, with that horrible leather toe. Nobody wears those. You can't feel anything in them. Buy ones made all out of satin. And very tight. They've got to fit very, very tight. If you need to pull the little strings, the shoes are too big."

I squeezed my long, narrow foot, normally a 7½AAAA, into a tiny pink 2½D. It is no easy matter, even for an expert in the field, to achieve an exact fit, especially for an elementary student; toe shoes are offered only in pre-decimal European sizes, which are quite a bit smaller than American ones. Shoes five sizes smaller (and more than half a dozen widths wider), such as I wore for some four years, are indeed extreme, but then, the cartilage never hardened properly between the bones in my feet; the time-honored methods of fitting weren't suitable for me. It took some years for the fruits of such foot-binding to manifest themselves; at the time, I was delighted.

What a toe shoe succeeds in doing is no less radical than changing the nature and function of the foot altogether. The leather backing and glue-stiffened toe block form an external bone structure, in principle not unlike a surgical corset or a crustacean's skeleton. The purpose is to support the underside of the arch and bind the toes together, thereby transforming them from five rather weak digits intended for delicate adjustments in balance into one solid digit strong enough to bear the entire weight of a body performing elaborate acrobatic tricks atop it.

Despite their importance in performance, toe shoes aren't worn by students every day. The majority of classes are given for and taken in soft shoes, either soft leather slippers much like those that gymnasts wear or old toe shoes with the heavy leather inner shank removed; pointe work is a finishing touch rather than a foundation. And men never wear toe shoes at all. The great Taglioni's father was right: pointe work calls for a precision of technique men are not physically capable of mastering. They cannot build force along slender lines as a woman can; the sheer weight and mass of muscle necessary to their brand of strength gets in the way of intricacy and speed.

At the Basic 4 level, I had one class on pointe a week; it lasted an hour and a half, which can seem a very long time when the skin of the toes is rubbing against a harshly textured, glue-stiffened brace. I wore no lamb's wool to lessen the friction; it wasn't done. Suki said so. "It makes you weak," she said. "And besides, you can't feel what you're doing." I could feel the blisters that resulted, though; they ranged from small white swellings of watery matter to half-dollar-size blood-filled bladders to the angry, bleeding subskin of the burst blister. After class, blood-stained tights and blood-soaked shoes were exposed and commented on. No tears were shed, but special fortitude drew special notice; the atmosphere was offhand Spartan. Suki taught me to cut away what remained of the blister's covering vesicle and sprinkle the subskin with a vicious, iodine-laden stuff called D.P.T. Powder. The pain was enough to make the victim giddy, but it was the custom, as Suki made plain, to perform the surgery publicly, soundlessly, in the waiting room along with fellow sufferers and assorted onlookers.

I doubt D.P.T. Powder was intended for the treatment of blisters, but it caused the exuding area to dry quickly, and that was what we wanted. In doing so, though, it formed a brittle covering of scarlike skin in which fissures opened up like red erosion marks in a dry lake bed. We treated these with D.P.T. Powder too; they healed more slowly, but the wounds remained uninfected, and the treatment, however radical, cleared the blister, however deep, in time for the following week's class.

There were other mysteries of a somewhat more minor character, but like toe shoes, they added to the esoteric nature of what I did in the afternoons. Some of the evidence of what I did—the exaggerated posture and peculiar walk I borrowed from Suki, the hardening muscles, the constant tiredness—was available for public comment like a skullcap or a rosary; the blisters and the sore thighs and the occasional strained tendon served notice to outsiders as the Ash Wednesday smudge on the forehead does. The nuances of dress, though, could be understood only by an insider.

I had worn all black at my first class, but I soon learned to discard it. Black was worn only by the less talented. Those who, like Suki, were gifted and known to be gifted wore pink tights and a leotard, either black or colored; at Suki's prompting I bought clothing suitable to my talents, which I assessed, again at her prompting, as considerable. But tights and leotard were only the beginning.

There are a number of supportive garments sold for dancers; the most common one for women at the time was a version of the male jockstrap, which all male dancers have to wear regardless of fashion. We disdained the jockstrap. Instead we wore baby pants, those very things designed to keep a baby's clothes dry when his diaper is wet. The ones we bought were completely airtight with the exception of holes through which safety pins were supposed to protrude, and they were pressed out of a single piece of rubbery plastic like a kitchen glove. We pulled them over our pink tights and stretched them dangerously—they often split when being put on or taken off—over our hips and bellies. Then we put on our leotards, which we tucked neatly into the leg openings of the plastic pants; the leg openings we rolled up to reveal just the right amount of interstice between outer thigh and pelvic bone, not too much (that was vulgar), not too little (that looked childish).

Baby pants made our bottoms look like extruded plastic basins, and they made sweat pour down our legs as though we, like the pants' intended users, had peed inside them. "They help keep fat off your hips," Suki told me, "and they make the line cleaner." I didn't know what she meant by line, and I was far too thin to be interested in losing weight, but I listened with attention and I did as she said.

Hair style had meaning too, although it was not so rigidly dictated. We usually wore a chignon, which we called a "rat." We bought special hair-colored nets to cover the chignon and special ribbons to decorate it. We always wore watches in class; Suki's was the tiniest mechanism I had ever seen, but my own was smaller than was good for the eyes. Earrings were out. Legwarmers were out.

The only pair of legwarmers I ever saw in San Francisco were on the first real professional dancer I ever saw anywhere at all, and I knew she wasn't a member of the San Francisco Ballet Company—none of whom I'd laid eyes on at the time—simply because she wore legwarmers. She took my class, Basic 4, one Saturday morning, but I knew she was a real professional even so, because Harold spent the entire barre talking to her. He didn't tease her, either; he used a polite, almost tentative tone, as though he were at a formal dinner party and she an honored guest. And except for the murmur of their voices—we could hear the heavy foreign accent in hers—the studio, always quiet, was unnaturally so during the entire class.

Until that Saturday, Suki was the most advanced dancer I'd seen close up; I'd thought she was what a real dancer looked like—rather like me, in fact—but Suki's turn-out was as yet only partially developed, and the sight of the full-blown balletic distortions of this new dancer made the skin crawl between my shoulder blades. Curly wisps of hair made a faint blond aureole around her square face, and her legs were so flexible that even when she stood normally they seemed partially disconnected at the hips and partially disconnected at the ankles; it didn't seem possible that anybody could control such limbs, but when she held her leg in second—out to the side of her body—it stayed there motionless, turned out to a complete profile, way up high in the air, as though obeying the strings of an unseen puppeteer. It was ugly and beautiful all at once, sinuous and strange, unnatural and yet consonant, powerful too, and almost other-worldly.

"Who *is* she?" I whispered to the girl next to me at the barre. "Why's she wearing those things on her legs?"

"Shhh," she said. And then, biting her lip, her voice full of awe, she said, "That's Violette Verdy. She's French."

She was, I learned from another friend in the dressing room after class, going through San Francisco on her way to New York; she'd danced leading roles in several European ballet companies and starred in two movies, and now she had a contract waiting for her at the American Ballet Theatre. I had a picture of her in one of my ballet books at home, and I studied it carefully for days afterward. But Suki never wore legwarmers even so. Nobody in the San Francisco Ballet School did. Legwarmers were out. And sweaters were out, no matter how cold the day.

Studying at school was in. Everybody who was gifted studied hard; it showed dedication. I found studying a disagreeable occupation. When Suki and I took the train to San Francisco together, I stared out the window daydreaming while she wrote rough drafts of essays in a large, untidy scrawl and memorized French verbs, her eyes closed and her small mouth working. I told her I would get motion sickness if I tried to write on the train. She said—not without scorn—that she didn't believe it.

"Look, Joanie," she went on, when I tried to press the point, "if you don't want to work, don't. But if I don't work, my grades will be as bad as yours. If you want to stare out the window, stare out the window. Whatever you do, don't talk to me about it. I've got to study."

So I watched her, and in the end I did as she did. I wrote when she wrote and read when she read and memorized when she memorized. Within weeks my grades were on a par with hers. During our sophomore year she and I got the highest marks given in geometry, and we were both honor students.

As often happens with people who enter a world closed to outsiders, I found my relationships with my family becoming somewhat strained. Judy and I had been taught from the time we were very small to talk openly about what we did and thought; it was our contribution to the Open Door Policy, and Mother used to quiz us frequently to ensure our adherence to our side of the bargain. Both our parents were forceful and opinionated, though; Judy and I learned early what we were expected to have thought and done, and like the docile children we were, we told our tales accordingly. We believed them ourselves too, the tales—most of them, anyway. We were not popular girls; we had few friends our own age, and until I met Suki no one of the few had been strong enough to tempt us out of the family orbit.

My mother took my exposure to the harshly unsentimental milieu of ballet particularly poorly; the tales I was prepared to blurt out were stripped of the niceties of middle-class society, and she seemed to waver between the certainty that I was growing corrupt and the fear that I was no longer quite right in the head.

"Guess what, Mother. Oh, guess what! Harold

asked me to demonstrate twice. Twice! I demonstrated at the barre and the pirouettes—"

"What does 'demonstrate' mean?"

"Well, you see, he gives an exercise and then he
asks somebody to do it all alone, to show the others,
and he—"

"Is that good?"

"It sure is. Suki usually does it."

"I thought she was in another class."

"She is, but she takes ours most days too."

"Why?"

"So she'll get stronger faster. You know, get better—"

"What's the hurry?"

"Oh, Mother, really! Now listen. The best part is—
oh, marvelous—she was there today. And it was *me*
who demonstrated. Twice. Isn't that divine?" "Divine" was a word all the gifted ones used.

"Good God, you're positively gloating."

"I should be. It's the very first time I've demonstrated when she's been there, and he said—"

"Was she upset?"

"Who?"

"Suki, of course. Who else?"

"I don't know—don't have any idea. The important
thing is that he said—"

"Joanie! Shame on you! Why don't you have any
idea? Don't you care?"

"Oh, Mother! I wasn't even looking at her. I was
demonstrating, and—"

"Don't you ever think of anybody else?"

"Who else? Suki? Are you still worried about—"

"Don't you ever think about anybody but Joan
Brady?"

And she didn't like the thoughts she sensed I
thought about myself, either. Mine was, she said, an
important age for a girl brought up under the Open
Door Policy. An exciting age. Pubic hair. Boys, perhaps. The menarche. Breasts. Sex emergent. Judy had

responded properly to all these beginnings only three years before. But my only discernible interest in pubic hair was how much of it had to be shaved off; I didn't want anything like that showing through my pink tights. I had little interest in boys; most boys weren't interested in ballet. And I saw the menarche as no more than a nuisance.

Judy discovered one day that I'd arrived; she found my blood-spotted underpants on the bathroom floor and carried them triumphantly to Mother, who exchanged a knowing smile with her. They both offered congratulations. We were three women together. But *I* knew that sanitary pads underneath baby pants soaked up sweat; from time to time, blood and sweat intermingled and tinged pink tights with red around the crotch. Black tights were a partial answer, but since the gifted ones didn't wear them, a once-monthly week in black served only as an advertisement. And then there wasn't enough time after class to change before the long and uncomfortable train ride home.

Breasts I wanted nothing to do with. When Judy was thirteen or so and I was about eleven, Mother used to joke about our breasts. "Look, Bob," she'd say, "Judy's got bee stings and Joanie's got mosquito bites." As for her own breasts, she felt only bitterness, and despite the dictates of the Open Door Policy, she rarely left them uncovered. "They used to be small, high and round," she told us, gesturing with her hands, "and now they sag down like udders. That's what breast-feeding does and I breast-fed both of you." Once, after a fight with my father, she said, her voice shaking with anger, "Bob said he didn't mind about my breasts. What right has he to mind or not to mind? What's it got to do with him? *I* don't mind his piebald penis."

When we were quite small, Mother used to gather Judy and me from the sandbox and lead us, a tiny and obedient procession, up the stairs to the bathroom so we could watch our daddy pee. This was somehow important to the Open Door Policy, as were the frequent and lengthy discussions of human reproduction, illustrated with full-color drawings in a medical book. "It's really so funny," Mother used to tell dinner guests. "Judy's eyes are glued to Bob's penis, and Joanie watches the water splashing in the bowl." I must admit I can remember being bored by the expeditions, but I had taken note of the piebald character of my father's penis even so. There was an irregularly shaped, strawberry-colored birthmark partially encircling the shaft; it bled up over the tip in an unexpected splash of gaiety on the otherwise dull quarter of flesh which occasioned those recesses from the sandbox.

My father said the mark had been caused by his circumcision, although it didn't look like a scar to me. He'd been circumcised at five on the kitchen table of his father's farm; the only light for the operation came from candles, the scalpel was a kitchen knife, and the surgeon was a vet too drunk to keep his hands steady. My father remembered the shadows flickering on the ceiling and the terrible pain; the fear of what might have happened came later and seemed, the one time I heard him speak of it, to cause him more distress than the memory itself.

By the time I was fourteen, my mother's joke about breasts had lost its savor. Judy, at almost seventeen, was plainly not going to make the standard, and I—to my horror—looked like growing beyond it. There was one big-breasted girl in the company, only one, and when she performed she had to bind her entire chest with surgical tape; by the end of a season her skin was coming off in patches. She was lucky, though; most big-breasted girls have to quit: the extra weight, appearing, as it usually does, after the center of balance has been long established, topples them forward. Besides, a dancer's body should be sleek; voluptuous figures belong elsewhere. I looked down at that foreign flesh growing on me, threatening my career even before it started, with nothing less than hatred.

As for sex in general, I had at an early age come to think of it mainly in terms of those chilly anatomical drawings and my urinating father; I couldn't see how either applied to me as a dancer, and I wasn't much interested in me as anything else—which wasn't, my mother said, shaking her head unhappily, a healthy state for a young girl to be in. At the ballet school, sex was discussed only in practical terms, along with baby pants, brands of sanitary pads, diet, blister preparations, and preferred material for bras and leotards; in fact, the whole business of growing up was divested, among my dancing acquaintances, of the uncomfortable mysticism that prevailed at home. And so I came, perhaps more quickly than might have been expected, to view the ballet school as a refuge—as a place, at any rate, particularly suited to me, where the signals were clear, where I understood the meanings of things.

3

Glissés, which follow *tendus battements* at the barre, are quick, sharp movements done at high speed to strengthen the biceps at the back of the leg; they build force for the complicated jumps and beats that are yet to come.

THE SHIFT in my allegiance from home to ballet school made me an alien in the family; from my partially outside vantage point I saw things I wasn't supposed to see and suffered from fears I couldn't vent. I knew that the nights when the reassuring sound of my mother's voice came through the wall into my room—she had a fine, deep, expressive reading voice and she read aloud to my father—were growing fewer and fewer. I knew that my father was sleeping more often in his study than he did in the parental bedroom. I knew the fights the two of them indulged in were taking over more and more of their time together. But the Open Door Policy, which admitted of differences of opinion strongly held, did not admit of increasing strain between parents, and Judy, whose world was still largely circumscribed by family law, saw nothing.

I knew especially that the sense of gloom which

ruled Sundays at our house was growing deeper. My
father hated Sundays. He always had. They had been
rigidly observed when he was a child; his father was a
fundamentalist preacher in a fire-and-brimstone sect
founded by himself. Every Sunday my father, his
brother and his five sisters had to recite a chapter of
the Bible at the breakfast table, and the old man beat
them with a strap if they faltered. Studying was strictly
forbidden on that day, and if my grandfather caught
them with any book other than the Bible, he beat them
with a strap. The old man conducted revivalist meet-
ings in a tent, and if no one came forth to be saved, it
fell to my father, as a boy, to confess publicly some
invented transgression and receive his own father's
blessing. The schoolkids, heads stuck under the tent
edge, watched and giggled, and the Mondays of teasing were, if anything, more horrifying than the Sundays that provoked them. If my father failed to come
forth to be saved, the old man beat him with a strap
until there was blood to wash away the transgression.
God, Jesus and my grandfather made up a triumvirate
that dealt out brutality and exacted public humiliation
in return. "I talk to Jesus every day," the old man used
to say, "and He talks to me."

When my father was ten or eleven, the old man told
him that if he defied God, God would strike him dead.
The next Sunday, out behind the barn, my father whispered, "God, I defy you." He waited a moment, steel-
ing himself, and then repeated the curse at the top of
his lungs. After that he had only one tyrant to deal
with, and the constant beatings, since their source was
no longer divine, were easier for him to bear; he
learned to hate then, and his hatred made the beatings
easier. But all through his life, Sundays called his
childhood memories together like a committee of
ghouls. The day was confined in walls dictated by the
past; his life's motto, "One slip of the foot and the
pack is at your throat," bore in on him hard, and he
courted Monday by going to bed as early as possible.

My father's Sunday moodiness worried my mother and hurt her too. She viewed her nature as a pragmatic one, straightforward, under control, almost dull, and she could not understand why, given such a nature, she failed to solace him. In fact she was temperamentally as flamboyant as he was. She had the easy sureness of manner good-looking people have, and she was intelligent, responsive, forceful, persevering, but she was also a changeable woman, possessive, easily stung, self-righteous, and given to sexual jealousies as profound in her as the faith in humankind to which she clung more and more tightly in the face of my father's increasing hatreds. And it was about this time that my father learned to talk with a cigarette hanging out of his mouth, the smoke curling up over his face and into his eyes. It gave him a raffish look which much became him; the wife of one of his colleagues smoked like that, and rumor had it that she had taught my father how.

But whatever it was precisely that caused the growing tension, the fights themselves seemed, at least to me, to be sparked by trifles, and when they occurred at night, exacerbated by alcohol. I sat in my room, listening to them, while I sewed ribbons on my toe shoes with tiny, regular stitches that were much admired at the San Francisco Ballet School for their exactitude if not for their strength.

But the ballet school itself, even though it functioned under the auspices of a dogma more reliable in its application and far more accessible to a novice than the Open Door Policy, was by no means without its unpleasant side. I had my guide in Suki, who was both willing and adept, but the school was, as she pointed out, set up to produce professional dancers. The staff there used whatever means were at hand to reach that end. Furthermore, she said, I had to view myself as an accomplice to them. I did want to be a dancer, didn't I? Well, then, that was that. Still, the harsh glare of such single-mindedness—mine and theirs combined—shook me sometimes and I was sometimes afraid.

As soon, for example, as I myself began to demonstrate exercises for the class under Harold's direction, I began to worry whenever someone else demonstrated. I used to watch whatever girl he chose—I wasn't upset when one of the boys demonstrated—fearing that perhaps her legs had a better shape than mine or her feet a prettier arch or her thighs a stronger turn-out. I was afraid I might have fallen out of favor or that my talent wasn't so great as I had imagined it to be. I turned these things over in my mind during the train rides to and from San Francisco, and I worried them at night when I was trying to sleep. Nobody at home seemed to have any idea what I was talking about, and I found the subject a difficult one to broach even with Suki.

But one day, unable to contain my uncertainties any longer, I said to her, "Suki, I don't think Harold wants me to be a dancer at all. Not really, I mean. Maybe he wants—"

"Why do you say that?"

"Well, he spent the whole time you were demonstrating saying things like 'Aren't her legs lovely and long, Joan? . . . Look at those feet, Joan; now there's a beautifully arched foot. . . . Do you see how well she closes into fifth?'"

Suki laughed. "He really works at it, doesn't he?"

"Works at what?"

"Oh, Joanie, don't you understand anything?" I shook my head; she sighed and went on patiently. "He just wants to make you jealous of me. He makes Eugenia jealous of Pam and Susan jealous of Eugenia and me jealous of Ginny Johnson and you—well, he tries to make you jealous of me."

"What for?"

"Oh, really, Joanie! To make you work harder, of course. Whatever else would be the point of it?"

"Well, he might be . . . just trying to teach me . . . how to become a teacher, like him . . . or something."

"Don't be silly. He wouldn't waste his time like that. He just wants to make you work harder. It's a compliment, really. Why don't you take it that way?"

I tried, and to some degree I succeeded. At least, I succeeded in becoming jealous of a number of girls, and I set out cold-bloodedly to beat them at whatever it was they did best. Suki nodded approvingly whenever I displayed evidence of such intentions, knowing, I'm sure, that it was she of whom I was the most jealous, and on behalf of the profession, approving these feelings too. She even said, much to my delight and her amusement, that she sometimes felt a little jealous of me; I did, after all, turn easily and I had a natural jump. But I didn't quite like the jealousy I felt; the element of fear was too strong in it. While it did make me work harder, it also made me more and more afraid of failure, and the fear of failure was growing stronger than the lure of success. Furthermore, I disliked the mélange of emotions that had come to govern a number of my friendships.

In class one winter evening, a girl who was a particular friend of mine fell with her leg bent at an uncompromising angle. The class froze, the music dwindled away, the pianist's haggard face appeared around the upraised cover of the grand, and the girl lay there on the floor like a beetle on its back, flailing her arms. While we watched, Harold examined her quickly, lifted her head onto his knee, and sent one of the boys to fetch Lew, his brother and the director of the company itself, whose class was in progress on the floor above. The girl rocked herself a little in Harold's arms, saying something—it was too faint for me to hear—over and over again in a singsong voice.

I'd never seen Lew before his hurried appearance in my classroom that evening, and without my glasses I could do little more than guess at his looks: blond, well-knit, aggressively male. He examined the girl with the quick, deft assurance of a professional, picked her up, nodded curtly to Harold, and carried her out of the room. His arms were muscular and slightly shiny in the artificial light.

"She said she was sorry," Harold said then, shaking his head in a puzzled way. "Her kneecap dislocated like that and she kept saying she was sorry. What could she have had in mind?" He sighed. "Well, now you know what happens if you turn out your feet and not your legs. The pressure has to go somewhere and—bang!—out goes the kneecap." He shook his head again. "She just kept saying she was sorry. Just that. I can't understand it." He shook his head once more, nodded to the pianist, who was always known as "Madame," and the class resumed.

"I don't think they were just being kind, Joanie," Suki said on the train as we were going home that night. "Poor old Harold probably couldn't understand why she wasn't blaming him." She paused a moment. "If she comes back, she'll have an edge. She wasn't too bad, was she? They'll pay more attention to her to make up for it. It'll be worth it to her in the end—a little pain, a month or two in a cast, and voilà! Most of the kids here would do it just to get carried away in Lew's arms. I wouldn't feel too sorry for her."

The girl never did come back. I don't know why. Even though she'd been a special friend of mine, I never telephoned to find out how she was. The fact is, I was afraid Suki's assessment would prove correct; she'd have an advantage over me—that girl, my friend—just because she'd fallen down and hurt herself. She was a sensitive girl, rather more openly friendly than most, rather less grim in her determination. I courted that grimness myself, but I preferred my friends without it, and so I was afraid, too, that she'd see resentment in my face. When, after a few months, it was clear she wasn't coming back after all, I was much relieved. Besides, Harold's attention had turned somewhat more in my direction during her absence; I wanted to keep it that way.

Harold Christensen, unlike his brother Lew, was not aggressively male. He was by no means effeminate, but he did not seem to have the need, as so many American men do, to wear his masculinity like a badge of merit. He had a narrow face, not handsome in the conventional manner but amused and appealing, with arched and tufted eyebrows and a tolerant expression. He was something of a ham. Preparing himself to demonstrate an exercise for us, he used to tilt his body backward from the waist like a clock at five minutes to six, pat his nonexistent belly fondly, shift his wide belt within its straps, tighten his feet into fifth position with a hula-inspired shimmy, lift his shoulders almost to his ears and settle them firmly into place with a noisy sigh. The faces around him remained unsmiling and serious during these antics, as though in the presence of divine revelation, and he used to look from one to the other of us, amused, or so it seemed, by our sternness in the face of his patent absurdity. He was built to too slender a pattern for a classical dancer, but he must have been a formidable comic, and despite the power he wielded—or seemed to wield—it was difficult not to like him. But I, along with most of the gifted ones, overcame that difficulty. In accordance with the creed of the school, I saw Harold as a means to an end; I fawned on him as the custom required; I hungered after his favors. And I despised him behind his back.

Suki danced with the company as an apprentice during the opera season; rehearsals and, later, performances in San Francisco kept her away from Anna Head's. She appeared some mornings with a trace of the black body paint she'd worn in *Aïda* only the night before still showing under her fingernails; there were excited flutters among the schoolgirls, and the jealousy she approved and Harold fostered grew in me vigorously. When the company went to Los Angeles, Suki went with them, and I began to wonder then how remote were the possibilities that she, like my other friend, might lose a kneecap.

I was left to myself on the train, with these thoughts scurrying at random among Euclid's propositions, which I was memorizing for my geometry class, and I carried them wholesale, Euclid and all, to bed with me at night, along with the midden of other fears I kept secreted away from the Open Door Policy. I seemed unable to rid myself of any of them; they clung to me while I tried to sleep. On the other side of the wall, my mother and father raged against each other in rising and falling rhythms that came to seem somehow geometric in form, too, as I listened.

In one of those childish attempts to ward off evil, I took to holding my breath as soon as I turned off the light, but the thoughts and the fights continued. Then one night I found I couldn't let my breath go naturally anymore; I had to monitor the intake, the retention and the expiration of air, and the monitoring took such concentration that I couldn't sleep at all. I became quickly exhausted, and during the day it seemed that I had to move my arms and legs with the same sense of artifice that pumping my lungs called for at night.

"She's overtired," the doctor said. "Nothing serious, but don't let it get out of hand. Take her away for a week—the desert or somewhere like that—and give her an ounce of bourbon before she goes to bed. Much better than tranquilizers."

"Is she having a nervous breakdown? Is that what it is?" My mother prided herself on being realistic in such matters.

"No, but she's a nervous girl—"

"Nervous? Highly strung, do you mean?"

The doctor shrugged. "—and she's got herself worked into a nervous state. A week in the desert and a nightly ounce of booze. That ought to fix her up."

In the desert a boy with red hair asked me to go swimming and my mother helped me with my Latin; the hot dry air dulled the intensity of my fears and jealousies, and the bourbon helped me to sleep. I came home rested and relaxed and anxious to get back to the ballet school. The desert must have been good for my parents too; for several weeks the fights at home were less frequent and, when they did occur, somewhat shorter in duration.

A dancer must learn to move her leg, held at a height above her own hip, in a perfect semicircle around her body; *ronds de jambe à terre* introduce this strange and difficult maneuver at the barre, with the working foot on the floor to develop the feel of it first before any real pressure is brought to bear.

MY MOTHER'S FATHER was a druggist, a quiet, gentle man with white hair and a beard; he loved my grandmother dearly despite her rages. She divorced him three times in the course of their life together, and he courted her four, beginning patiently each time with roses and chocolates and chaperoned evenings; he married her four times too, three of them in church with bridesmaids and only the last in the registry office. She had been a genuine beauty, my grandmother—high cheekbones, almond eyes, oval face, very fair—and she'd run away from home at twelve; by the time she was thirteen she was making her living as a telegraph operator. At twenty she met my grandfather; at twenty-one she married him. During their honeymoon, they went on a picnic with another couple; my grandmother and her friend walked in long skirts behind the two young husbands, who were carrying wicker baskets of sandwiches and fruit and lemonade. My grandfather's hair was black then and my grandmother, looking at him from behind, noticed dandruff at the nape of his neck and she loathed him for it. The loathing stayed with her, in her bed at night, through three pregnancies and the rearing of three children, three divorces and three remarriages, into old age, when she still thought she could see dandruff at the nape of his neck even though his hair was white and her eyesight poor. But he loved her, that she knew, and she understood the value of it.

My mother, her firstborn, cried a lot and contracted all available childhood diseases in her first year; my grandmother threw her across the room once and would have thrown her back again if my grandfather hadn't restrained her. My mother could never quite forgive her that violence, although she could not remember it herself and although she used to tell Judy and me the story with a touch of pride, as the survivor of an ordeal.

Despite that stormy beginning, my mother's childhood was uneventful; the family was, as one of her younger brothers put it, rather "drab," with the exception of that peculiar pattern of divorces and remarriages. My mother loved school and did well in it, grew very pretty, enjoyed considerable popularity, got herself tossed out of college for publishing a forbidden newspaper, married her first Irishman, Sean Forsyth, and moved with him to New York to seek her fortune. There she went to work on *Theatre Arts* magazine, flirted with the idea of being an actress, divorced Sean, who drank too much, and went to work for a new trade magazine called *Tide*—begun by *Time* but sold shortly thereafter to the advertising agent Raymond Rubicam, who took as its editor a twenty-two-year-old then writing book reviews and bits and pieces for *Time*. His name was Dexter Masters; my mother met him when she was looking for a job and he was looking for someone to help him get his magazine going; he hired her and they worked closely together for the next five years. There was talk of marriage, but he didn't want to have children and she did, and about then she met her second Irishman, Robert Brady, who became my father. He wasn't able to marry her, either; his first wife refused to divorce him, and so my mother and he moved to California, where Judy and I were born bastards. She and I didn't really grasp these details until much later: the Open Door Policy showed flexibility in matters of sentiment. "Bob and I don't celebrate our wedding anniversary like most people," my mother used to say. "We celebrate the day we decided to get married."

Sean Forsyth dwindled into a story-time name, but Dexter Masters remained my mother's active friend, and over the years that followed, my father became almost as fond of him as my mother was herself. They wrote frequently, my mother and Dexter, supported each other in times of need—both emotional and financial—and he visited us at our house in Berkeley. He was tall and dark—dark hair, almost black, and dark eyes—slender and very good to look at; his manner was never condescending, he amused me, and I fell in love with him when I was three. "No, no, Joanie," my mother used to say, laughing. "You can't have him. He's going to be the husband of my old age. It's all arranged."

As for me, I did not find the joke altogether funny. My intent was serious, and it remained so. I had to concede, of course, that the prospect of my marrying anybody while I still wore puff sleeves and a sash had its incongruous side, but later on, looking at the matter with a ballet student's critical eye, I decided my mother's prettiness showed signs of fading. She was in her middle forties already; I figured I would stand a chance when the time came.

In the meantime there was Walt Huron. Walt was fourteen, as I was, and the only talented boy in Basic 4. I had eyed him curiously from time to time, aware that he was already rehearsing minor roles with the company and so by rights could have little interest in such as me. One day, however, he chose a place next to me at the barre, and just before class started, peeled off one of the three Band-Aids that adorned his left arm.

"See?" he said.

I peered nearsightedly at the still suppurating wound offered for my view. "Oh," I said.

"Hurts a little."

"Oh."

"Wanna see another?"

I nodded timidly, and he peeled off a second Band-Aid. The wound beneath looked infected. "Oh!" I said.

He grinned. "This one hurts a little too, but not so much as the other. And *that*"—he pointed at one of the several brown-black raised areas on his biceps— "that's the one that'll go next."

"Oh."

"I do it myself. I got shingles, see? I cut them out with a nail file. You got to dig it out, you know, scrape it clean and then pour alcohol in the hole."

"Oh!"

He smiled proudly, and we studied his arm together. Then he restuck the Band-Aid and there was an awkward pause.

"And what's under *that* one?" I asked suddenly, pointing to the third Band-Aid. Walt blushed. I blushed. We both laughed, and we were friends.

Walt had brown hair that curled gently at the nape of his neck and brown eyes a little like Dexter's; his body was well formed and his feet sturdy but elegantly arched. His mother had carried him almost eleven months before giving birth to him, and that was why, so he told me, he looked much older than he was. He had, at only fourteen, a moderately well-established beard; his shoulders were broad, his full height plainly reached, his voice changed. Underneath his tights, the wad at his crotch was truly formidable. He said he needed to be so grown-up-looking because he had to fight at school to prove his masculinity. I used to ask about his school friends while we sat in a drugstore not far from the ballet school, drinking coffee and listening to the jukebox.

"Well, it isn't easy. In the first place, I'm intelligent. Very intelligent. My IQ is the highest in the school, and they don't like that. I get good grades without trying, and they don't like that. *And* I take ballet lessons. Now, that's something they can get hold of. So I have to fight. But since I'm bigger and stronger than they are, I win. And they don't like that." He sighed. "I don't really have any friends at school."

"What about the girls? Aren't they friendly, either?"

"The only girl I can talk to is you."

We did a lot of talking. We talked about the meanings of things and we agreed. We talked about dancing and we agreed. We talked about people, and we agreed there too, although Walt had fears that I only barely understood. "Don't let them crush you, Joan," he used to say. "Don't let them get at you. They'll try, you know, and I'll break the neck of anybody who— But by then it's too late, isn't it?" His whole body trembled with intensity when he danced and when he talked about such matters; every now and again he reached out, trembling, as though to touch my fingers across the table, but each time he withdrew, still trembling, without having done so. Once or twice, on the way back from the drugstore to the ballet school, the knuckles of his hand brushed against me as though by accident while he looked steadfastly at the view out over the bay.

He went with the company on its spring tour, and he bought himself a gold ring with the first hundred dollars he earned; with the next fifty dollars he bought a gold chain. When he got back, we went to the drugstore for coffee together, and he presented me with the ring, hung on its chain. I bowed my head, and gently, with gravity and deliberation, he placed the chain around my neck. He sat down opposite me then and, smiling, touched the very tip of his index finger to the very tip of mine.

I wore the chain every day, and at school girls sought me out for consultation in matters of the heart; I was the first in our class to go steady. One or two asked me what it was like to be kissed, and my blush was interpreted as evidence of abandon; I pretended to discretion, and the pretense served only to increase my reputation. Walt's mother sent me a note written on a small piece of lavender paper in a crabbed hand, asking me to come to tea.

Walt and I walked to his house together, and on the way he told me that he had been the last of his mother's six pregnancies. There had been five stillborn brothers and sisters, and when his mother was in labor the last time, the doctors had come to his father and said, "We can save the baby or the mother, but not both. Which do you want?" Walt's father begged them to save his wife, and Walt, who had proved tougher than they thought, said he could never forgive that. "It's a hard thing to bear," he said, "to know your parents didn't want you from the moment you were born. How can I forgive a thing like that?"

The living room was very small, the furniture faded, large, overstuffed, the walls pale green and a little grimy, the windows shaded. Walt's mother had baked a chocolate cake, and she sat on the edge of a huge divan, half hidden by a heavy mahogany bureau that loomed out into the room; she held her head cocked apologetically to one side and sipped tea out of a cup with an elaborate floral design. Her teeth clattered audibly against the china. Walt's father sat beside her massaging the knuckles of his right hand; after a few minutes he leaned over to me and said in a stage whisper, "She's kinda nervous, see, on accounta your being a professor's daughter." He winced, looked down at his hands, and massaged harder. "A professor's daughter, see? She's not used to that." I nodded. "Too nervous even to eat some of her own cake. Don't often have home-baked cake. Too nervous for it, see?" I nodded. "It ain't good for her to be alone in the kitchen. She don't bake unless I'm here to kinda—well, make sure. See?" I nodded.

Walt shifted in his chair; his mother pulled herself a little farther behind the mahogany bureau. "Walt's a good boy," his father went on. "Ain't you, Walt? Dancing's a good profession. Say what they like. It's regular. Not like me, see?" I nodded. "You gotta be in a union to paint regular. I ain't got no union. On my own, see? Job lots of paint. Prewar, sometimes, full of lead. Landlord says to me, 'Any color. Whatever you got. Just make it cheap.' No dough in that. And lead hurts you sometimes. Blue gums, see?" He pulled down his lower lip and jutted his face toward me, but I couldn't see much in the dim light of the room. "You don't get hurt dancing. Right, Walt? Money's not bad. I looked into it. Got a union even. Mother don't complain, but maybe I get sick sometimes—after a big job, see?—and she don't know what to do. Call a doctor; he just says I gotta stop. So how am I gonna do that? Who's gonna take care of Mother then? I don't know nothing else. But dancing—well, like I say, it's regular, Miss, and my boy—"

"It's Joan!" Walt hissed at him. "Her name's Joan."

"Yeah," he went on. "They give him a scholarship to learn dancing. I ain't got the dough to send him anywhere to learn a job. But up there—that dancing school—they told me. He learns for free. And he has a profession when he's learned. Good money. Regular. And a union card. Go places, too. Who else's gonna offer my boy that?"

I've always been afraid of the dark. It's not the natural disasters, the robbers and rapists and whatever, that worry me; it's the supernatural things: the faint, uneven footsteps that no foot is making; the barely audible sound of breath when there isn't any breather.

The night my father tried to kill himself the unnatural quiet of the house was alive with menace of that sort. The fights he and my mother indulged in had a familiar rhythm; I had become accustomed to going to sleep to them, and there was no silence in the pattern. Risings and fallings of anger, but no silence. I was already out of bed, standing in the dark of my room, filled with alarm, when my mother's voice broke the queer stillness that had awakened me.

"Let me in, Bob! Let me in!" Her shout was almost a scream, and I'd never heard her scream before. "What are you doing in there?"

I crept to my door and peeked out; down the hallway from me, Judy peeked out from her door. I continued creeping until we sat together in her room.

"Let me in. Open the door. Oh, please." A pause. "Dammit, Bob, open that door." Another pause. "Judy! Judy! Go get Donald! Now!" Mother stood framed in the open doorway to her bedroom. She was entirely naked—not even a T-shirt to cover the unhappy breasts—and there were red welts rising here and there on her body. "Tell him to bring the crowbar. Fast!"

Judy ran. Donald lived in the basement; our father had fixed up a small apartment there and he let it out to students of his in exchange for a few hours of gardening a week. Our yard was almost an acre and elaborately landscaped; there was too much weeding for one man. Donald hated vegetables, but he had talent as an economist and he wasn't too bad with weeds. We were all very fond of him.

Edging toward my parents' bedroom, I could see Mother pulling clothes over her head. By the time Donald arrived, she was dressed; he stood behind her—a tall, thin young man with an Easter Island face—self-conscious with crowbar in hand.

"Bob, please, Donald has a crowbar here and we're going to break down that door unless you open it right now. Bob? Do you hear me? Please."

No answer. Silence. My mother nodded, and Donald inserted the crowbar near the lock of the door; he was strong despite his leanness, and the door splintered at the first thrust. The light in the bathroom shone white; beyond my mother and Donald I could see my father, upright and elegant in the red robe my mother had bought him; he stood quietly in front of the mirror, not moving at all, just looking at himself. There were pieces of splintered door all about; the heavy folds of the robe—a silk paisley brocade, plum, lake-red, and crimson—hung almost to his ankles. My mother wept. Judy and I gawked. Donald fell to his knees and started picking up pills from the bathroom floor. My father stood still in the middle of all the activity, absolutely still, looking into the mirror.

I don't remember who called the police, and I don't remember the two uniformed men arriving. But they must have arrived very quickly, because my father showed no signs of drowsiness at all as he took them into the living room, where my mother awaited them; he offered them a seat and sat himself down in a large chair, his face wholly composed, his manner indulgently arrogant. The policemen were ill at ease. Doubtless the imperial robe and its wearer intimidated them, one comically fat and short, the other awkwardly angular and shy; doubtless the situation was not at all what the telephone call had led them to expect. Judy and I watched from the darkened kitchen.

"There's no truth in it whatever," we heard our father say. "None at all. You can see for yourselves. The woman's hysterical."

His voice had just the right mix of professional sarcasm and conspiratorial contempt; my mother's eyes were red and her hastily put-on clothes in disarray. I don't know what had happened to Donald, but he wasn't there. The policemen looked nervously from my mother to my father and back again.

"Look," my mother said in her deep, lovely voice, "listen to me. He took dozens of pills. My father's a druggist. He got a bottle of five hundred from him. Barbiturates. It was a new bottle. Never opened before—"

"Oh, really, Mildred. Isn't it enough for you to have gotten these men out in the middle of the night for nothing?" He turned to the two policemen and smiled. "My wife has a tendency to fantasize."

"Well, sir, do you, uh, think we should—"

"For God's sake," my mother broke in, "look for yourselves if you don't believe what I say. Come upstairs and look." She took hold of the awkward policeman's sleeve, and he blushed. But he went with her, and a few minutes later he called for his partner. By the time they returned to the living room, my father's control was slipping.

An ambulance was summoned: stretchers and men in white. They removed the beautiful red robe with professional efficiency, but my father refused to mount the stretcher. He stumbled out to the ambulance in his white T-shirt, bare-bottomed and drunken, between two attendants. The fat policeman stayed awhile with Judy and me. We offered him coffee, and when he refused, Judy got out her cigarettes and offered him one of those, which he took. Seeking order where I felt surest, I extracted needle and thread from my hatbox, and stitched ribbons onto a new pair of toe shoes; I was experimenting at the time with a new and stronger stitch. I had great hopes for it.

5

During fondus *the coordination essential to the elaborately patterned jumps of ballet undergoes, at the barre, a minute dissection—a rehearsal in slow motion, so to speak, of what the future holds.*

MY FATHER MADE medical history in California; he broke all their records. Pumped from his stomach was an estimated five hundred grains of Nembutal, and at the end of a coma lasting almost three weeks his body took on the splotchiness of death. The nurse in attendance at the time was a Catholic; noting his patient's Irish name, he administered extreme unction. "He was practically dead," the nurse told us afterward. "I'd have called a priest, but you see, for all practical purposes he *was* dead. I was afraid I was too late anyway."

With the hurriedly sanctified oil on his palms and forehead, my father suddenly turned healthy pink. He'd ruined his kidneys and permanently raised his blood pressure, but he lived. Nobody understood how. The nurse's faith in holy sacrament deepened. My mother decided a Protestant soul had returned from hell in indignation at those last rites; my father was, after all, the son of a fundamentalist preacher and the son of the son of an Orangeman. The hospital, which had announced his death to the local newspapers, was simply embarrassed. Two obituaries appeared. Those were the McCarthy days, and both stories were more concerned with the un-American opposition my father had put up against Berkeley's loyalty oath than with his death or his achievement as an economist. He found them amusing reading during his long convalescence; they reassured him that the world was intact and that his assessment of its inhabitants as a pack of wolves was the correct one.

Even before he was off the critical list he wanted to come home. He wept like a child when the visiting hours were over; no one could console him. He had lost a great deal of weight during his coma, and in his unhappiness he began to lose more. He didn't want to eat; if forced, he vomited. After some six weeks the doctors decided he would die if he stayed. My mother fixed up the dining room with a hospital bed that raised and lowered and had sides to make it into a gigantic crib at night; there was a chart stuck to the metal railing at the foot for daily records of liquid intake and output, blood pressure, pulse, temperature. The dining room table stood by one wall, covered with the accoutrements of the sickroom; thermometers, kidney-shaped bowls, dismantled hypodermic, medical tableware, urinal and bedpan under white towels, black rubber blood pressure gauge, flasks and vials. For the first month the doctor came every day and sometimes twice; at night a psychiatric nurse sat by the bedside. My mother made broth and milk toast and custard and fed my father biteful by biteful. In the afternoons she held his hand while he slept. It was summertime. Little by little he got stronger.

School was out; I had only one ballet class a day, and so I used to read to him as he lay there—Tennyson and Arnold— and I used to put an occasional concerto on the record player. The poetry made tears run down his cheeks and the music did the same; he remained bedridden throughout July and half of August, and he had that musty smell sick people have. With the approach of September he rallied. The nurse was dismissed. One night he managed to climb the stairs and find his way into my mother's bed; the hospital equipment was sent away. He read the newspapers in the morning, ordered spring bulbs for the yard, began to work out his fall courses. During the last two weeks of September, my mother took him to Hawaii so he could get some sun and a change of scene before the university's fall term began. That's what she told Judy and me anyway. On their return, we noticed she wore a heavy gold ring on her left hand, but we didn't pay much attention to it. They were both dead before we found out that the Hawaiian trip had celebrated their marriage, our legitimization, and my father's entry into the field of bigamy.

With the end of summer, too, the San Francisco Ballet began rehearsals for the opera season; at the time, the San Francisco Opera was the only international company in the country outside New York, and the San Francisco Ballet owed its financial existence to its position as ballet to the opera. I was called from class one day and told to attend all rehearsals for *Aïda:* I was to be an understudy. My friend Alicia Slater was to be an understudy too, and we could hardly contain ourselves. Jealousy was heavy in Basic 4, which had been upgraded at the beginning of the new school term to Advanced 1—and the jealously gave Alicia and me almost as much pleasure as the privilege that had provoked it. We withdrew ourselves a little. We were neither of us yet fifteen; there were many in our class who were older than we, and in their opinion more worthy. Tears were shed in the dressing room.

As for the rehearsals themselves, they confused us both. They were held in the upstairs studio, where the advanced and professional classes usually took place, a huge, wood-paneled room with a rich, dark feel to it despite its ample light and its wall of mirrors. Lew, distant, imperious and frightening, told us in an off-hand manner that we were to learn the priestesses' dance in the temple scene and the corps part in the triumphal scene. But he told us no more, and we didn't have any idea how to go about the mysterious business of learning the parts of some sixteen dancers. To be sure, all sixteen were doing more or less the same thing, but that "more or less" puzzled us greatly. We couldn't remember who went in front or in back of whom and when, and we didn't have the wit to realize that such interweaving was less important than the steps that were being interwoven. It never occurred to either of us to pick one dancer, learn her part first and worry about adjustments later. But then, stringing together more steps than we could remember at once seemed to present grave and—to us—almost insurmountable difficulties, anyway; the longest sequence of steps we'd learned were class exercises. The company members already knew their parts, so that no gradual learning process went on, and no one was given the job of seeing that we learned what we were there to learn. We were happy, though, just to be there, just to test the air, just to tell our school friends that we had to get out of lessons early to attend opera rehearsals. Besides, nobody in the San Francisco Ballet ever got sick.

Late in the afternoon of the opening night, when *Aïda* was to have its only performance of the season, both Alicia and I felt a little depressed. No company class was to be held in the upstairs studio; all the dancers were at the opera house. There were to be no more rehearsals. We dressed for class in silence. During the *pliés,* Harold stood beside me, as he often did with pupils he liked, and asked me with some amusement if I was going to miss the rehearsals. I nodded and smiled.

"You enjoy them, do you?" I nodded. "Would you like to do more of them?" I nodded vigorously. "Well, then," he said, "I have a surprise for you. Tonight you are to perform in the temple scene. Don't look so alarmed. I'm not joking. But you must hurry now. Run along. Get down to the opera house as fast as you can. They'll give you directions at the stage door."

There was a pause. I swallowed and managed to say, "Leave class?"

He laughed. "That's right. Go on now. Hurry!"

I don't remember arriving at the War Memorial Opera House, and I don't remember asking anybody how to get anywhere. I do remember climbing up the iron fire escape, to the fifth floor, where the youngest dancers dressed, and I remember the smell of sweat and body paint, the sense of rush, the sound of foreign languages, the tuning up of violins and sopranos. And I remember the fear. I certainly remember that. Somebody found me a costume, a pretty costume of gauzy white material with fine, narrow pleats hanging from an Empire bodice. Somebody showed me how to apply body paint to my arms and back and legs and neck. Somebody loaned me facial makeup and somebody helped me put it on. Somebody found me a headdress and a black wig, and somebody made sure both fitted and were secure. But I was too frightened to tell one somebody from the other somebodies; myself in the mirror looking exotic beyond my wildest dreams had more the quality of a nightmare in which the end of the tunnel closes over than of the fulfillment I was sure I would have felt if only I had had some sort of hold on the steps.

A somebody took me down to the fourth floor, where the older dancers dressed. There, out on the landing of the iron staircase, the girl whose part I was to perform spoke to me gently. She was perhaps eighteen and her knees, she told me, were too painful for the long kneeling sequence the temple scene demanded. A sudden, acute arthritis, hopefully transient, she said. She walked me through my part, quietly, patiently, two or three times; but my head was frozen. I couldn't keep anything in it.

The orchestra began to tune up. The sound of it erupted through the speakers that fed into all dressing rooms and backstage hallways. It was an ancient system; it hissed and crackled, and beyond the scattered arpeggios of strings and woodwinds, the audience talked, rustled, laughed, coughed. I suddenly had to pee, and very badly, too. Scrambling upstairs to the fifth floor, hand at crotch, I reached toward the toilet seat as a dehydrated desert rat might reach toward an oasis. But I did so only to manage the most meager of trickles. I could not understand it, and my puzzlement momentarily overcame my fear. The anonymous somebodies merged for that lucid interval into Suki, blacked all over, dressed as a miniature minstrel in gold bangles and red pantaloons; she helped me back into my costume, commenting with professional aplomb on the vagaries of stage fright and the illusions it produces. But before she had me hooked up again, the opening bars of the overture crackled through the speaker, and the desire returned, as abrupt and fierce as it was absurd. This time the results were entirely negative.

Halfway down the metal staircase to what I viewed in my heart as the place of execution, I had to pee again, and the illusion persisted; my legs began to tremble, and no matter how hard I tried, I could not remember a single sequence of steps. I waited in the wings, teeth chattering, shifting from foot to foot. Men in overalls rushed and people in lavish costumes lounged. I was in the way. "Out! Out!" "Jesus Christ! These goddamned babies they use here!" "Move, kid. Fast." The priestesses assembled slowly off to one side where it had not occurred to me to go. I half joined them, lingering at the edge of the group for a moment, shifting still from foot to foot in what seemed unendurable agony, before I could bear it no longer. I bolted for the fire escape staircase. And ran into Lew.

He grabbed my arm and frowned. "Where the hell are you going? You're on next." I opened my mouth to say something, but only a dry-sounding squawk came out. "Look," he said, peering suspiciously into my face—he'd never spoken to me personally and I wasn't sure he even knew my name—"you do this and you do it right. Or I'll shoot you." He swung me around and pushed me in the direction of the wings.

The curtain was down when we filed onto the stage. I was both pleased and surprised; our entrance had worried me considerably. At the rehearsals there hadn't seemed to be any entrance, and I was too shy or not enough interested to ask what actually happened. Once at the opera house, I had simply been too afraid. We knelt in a semicircle, each grasping a dimly lit lamp, and another mystery was explained; over a cup of coffee one afternoon Alicia and I had wondered idly and to no solution why the hands were held in such an odd position before the dance began. I found, understanding these things, that I could remember the opening steps of the dance itself, although I had never rehearsed it from the downstage left position Lew had put me in, and I had no idea just when we were supposed to begin.

The kneeling lasted a long time. I can remember peeking over my lamp from time to time to make sure I hadn't been left behind, and I can remember that the fear came and went in waves. But most of all I remember Nancy Johnson. Nancy was the San Francisco Ballet's leading dancer at the time, and I and all my peers worshiped her. She wasn't strong technically; any corps dancer in the New York City Ballet and practically any in the San Francisco Ballet could handle steps she faltered on. But she was a remarkable performer. On stage—and off, for that matter—she had the almost threatening sensuality usually associated with such male actors as Marlon Brando. In an art all too often identified with sexless femininity,

Nancy embodied the primeval female, relaxed, sure, languid, with the long muscles, the animal grace and the careless contempt of a cat; she managed to dance even so ladylike a role as the Sugar Plum Fairy with an erotic undercurrent that gave Lew Christensen's *Nutcracker*—otherwise a pretty silly piece of work—something of the rare and strange. And in the darkness of the priestesses' temple, she knelt next to me.

Because the company was small, Nancy took on corps roles when the numbers weren't sufficient, and after we had knelt together while Radames made his appeal to the gods, I heard her say, "Now, Joan!" Her voice was deep and well-modulated, in keeping. "Begin to rise now. That's it. Not so quick. Left foot forward. Right arm to the front. Very slow. Watch out for your lamp; you don't want to trip. . . ." And the voice continued throughout, calm, reassuring, always there.

6

The aim of a *frappé* is to achieve something akin to a panic reaction in the thighs, but to achieve it under controlled circumstances; the dancer memorizes her achievement at the barre for use later on when the just barely suppressed muscular excitement will lend an edge to whatever she does.

THE SAN FRANCISCO BALLET SCHOOL moved premises in the spring; the new school was located way out along Geary Street, not far from Golden Gate Park and the beach beyond. The Christensen brothers had bought an old garage and refitted its upper story with sprung hardwood flooring; three huge rooms stood in a row there, each of them large enough for a class of forty to fifty students, each of them well lit and mirrored, each divided from the next by soundproofed folding doors which could be opened to make a small theater with a raised stage—the floor of the third and last studio was some six feet above the others—an orchestra pit and a modest gallery.

The dressing rooms were on the ground floor, the boys to one side and the girls to the other, company and students combined; both rooms had showers, lockers, wash basins and rows of toilets. A waiting room separated them. Toward the front of the building

64

lay offices for Lew and Harold, a desk with a receptionist, and a second waiting room, for parents, guests and other outsiders. The back reaches, behind the dressing rooms, served as store for costumes and scenery and the like. We all agreed that it was a marvelous place.

All except the homosexuals in the company, that is. They disappeared, along with the old secretary, who used to paint her fingernails at her desk. According to Suki, Lew wasn't upset at either loss, despite the fact that the men's ranks, always meager, became alarmingly so that year: the company's best partner gone, its best actor too. She told me it wasn't the first time dancers had simply disappeared.

Just before I'd started taking classes there, she said, the company had been much bigger. Without warning, Lew had dropped a dozen or so dancers he no longer wanted. He didn't say anything to them; their names simply ceased to appear on the rehearsal lists, and they drifted away of their own accord. "Convenient for him, wasn't it?" she said. "The company was much better afterward, though. Much."

At the old school on California Street, the company and the advanced students had dressed and waited for classes on the other side of the building, well away from the less advanced pupils. As one grouped with the gifted girls, I had enjoyed a privileged position from the first, and my friendship with Suki had given me a certain éclat. With the move to Geary Street, I was promoted to Advanced 1A, the class just below the company class that Suki was taking, and my peers saw, too, because of the communal waiting room, that members of the company knew me by name. Nancy Johnson herself was heard to say, "Hello, Joan." And I wore Walt's ring around my neck as well; most of the other girls had thought Walt something of a fool before he'd actually joined the company, but a member of the company was, after all, a member of the company. Girls who had paid me little attention before sought me out for advice on blisters and diets, and I was greeted warmly when I walked through the door. It was not a situation I had had much experience with.

Things were not like that at Anna Head's. One lunch hour, I'd walked into a room to find Suki facing half a dozen of our classmates, all of whom fell silent when they saw me. She chewed on a chicken leg she held in her hand. Everybody waited, watching her, while she cracked the bone with her small, sharp teeth and sucked at the marrow inside. She licked her fingers then and turned to the assembled group. "You're stupid," she said. "All of you. Just stupid. Come on, Joanie, let's get out of here."

"Look, darling," my mother said, when I told her about it later, "it's probably just that they want to talk about themselves and not about you. Nothing interests people as much as talk about themselves. You've got to learn a little give and take, that's all."

"You don't know what I talk to them about."

"Yourself, obviously. You're no different than they are, you know."

I gathered up my coat and walked to Suki's house, which stood high up in the Berkeley hills, a mile or two from our own.

"What were they saying, Suki?" I asked. "Tell me."

"They're stupid," she said, handing me a Kleenex to wipe away the tears. "They don't know anything."

"Tell me."

She shrugged. "They say you *think* you're so talented as a dancer—"

"But I never talk to them about ballet. Not ever."

"Sure. So they say you're stuck up."

"In short, they don't like me. Any of them."

"Well," she said, "you *mind* so much. I don't think they really like me, either, but since I don't give a damn they get worried. You care. You show it on your face. And your hands too; you fiddle with them."

I'd always fiddled with my hands, and I wrapped my legs around the legs of chairs and tapped my feet on

floor. At the breakfast table I used to watch while
father turned a slow red around the cheeks. "God-
mn it, Joanie!" he'd shout when he could bear it no
nger. "Will you stop that endless jiggling? You're
iving me crazy." As for my mother, "You can't lie to
e, Joanie," she said more times than I can remember.
Your face gives away everything that goes on inside
ou. You're the only person I know who needs no
ords to speak with."

"Anyhow," Suki went on, "I told them you had a
holarship at San Francisco, and that shut them up."
I laughed. "Did they believe you?"
"What difference does it make? It's true."
"No it's not, Suki."
"Of course it is." I shook my head. "You must have
e," she said. "It's just that you don't know about it."
"My mother complains every month when she
rites out the checks. I know."
"But look, Joanie, everybody who's talented has
e. I have one. Eugenia has one. Pam has one. Tillie
s one. You should have one. If you don't get one
ou won't go into the company as quickly—"
"Why not?"
She sighed. "Because they need money more than
ey need talented girls. If you're paying and someone
ot quite so good as you isn't, they're going to take the
omeone who isn't quite so good before they take you,
o they can still get your money each month. It's just
ommon sense. You've got to get one."
"How?"
"Just tell them you can't pay anymore. Have your
other call them up and tell them that. That's all there
to it."
"Suppose they said, 'O.K., too bad'?"
"They won't. Don't be silly. You must have some
dea of your own worth."
Suki had a good idea of her own worth. That spring
he agreed to perform the title role in a recital put on
y a fairly large ballet school in Oakland; I offered to

make her costume. I sewed quite well. She was [t]
wear an elegant tutu with an imitation-gold-lamé bo[d]
and she came for numerous fittings at my house. S[he]
sometimes spent the night; whenever she did, we [lis]
tened to ballet records after dinner. On the night of h[er]
last fitting—the costume was both regal and delica[te]
and despite her businesslike air she plainly liked t[he]
look of herself in it—we took *Swan Lake* out of t[he]
record cabinet. We had listened to it many times b[e]
fore; I liked parts of it, but mainly I listened becau[se]
she did.

She closed her eyes while the music played, a[nd]
clutched her thin hands togther so tightly that I cou[ld]
see white around her knuckles. The muscles in h[er]
cheeks worked; I was at first puzzled and then restiv[e.]
Her tension seemed to reach a peak during the sw[an]
queen's solo music, and I said, growing somewh[at]
alarmed, "Suki, what's the matter?"

She opened her eyes a moment later, when the so[lo]
was finished, and spoke through clenched teeth; h[er]
voice was low and almost gravelly. "That should b[e]
me."

I had never seen her in such a mood. "What shoul[d]
be you? The music? What are you talking about?"

"No, not the music. Of course not." She shook h[er]
head irritably. "The part. Don't you see? The part [is]
mine. It's me. Mine."

My mother refused outright to apply for the schola[r]
ship. She was not going to throw herself on the charit[y]
of the brothers Christensen. It was dishonest, she sai[d,]
and it had nothing whatever to do with my work. Be[-]
sides, there wasn't any hurry about getting into th[e]
company. School came first. Suki had her father ca[ll]
and explain. I pleaded and begged.

"It's just money," my mother said. And each mont[h]
she complained as she wrote out the check.

The money she spent on my behalf was not m[y]
father's alone. She earned too—not steadily, but ofte[n]
more than he did—as an expert in the field of con[

umer economics. She was a thoroughly professional
journalist who at one time or another wrote on a va-
ety of subjects for *Theatre Arts, Harper's, New Re-
ublic, McCall's* and other publications. But from her
arly days at *Tide* magazine with Dexter Masters,
he'd made herself an unusual specialist in advertising
nd marketing matters, at first from a trade point of
iew but increasingly as a consumer advocate, an
arly Ralph Nader of genuine fire and effectiveness.
he had joined with Dexter and my father to help
ound Consumers Union; and as the first editor of *Con-
umer Reports,* Dexter had got her to start up a West
oast office of Consumers Union, which she was run-
ing in the very year I was born. At the time of my plea
or a scholarship and her refusal to request it, she was
oing the investigative work that led a few years later
o the truth-in-lending bill which became U.S. statute
rgely due to her efforts.

Her relations with Dexter were obviously numerous
nd durable, but just what they took in precisely—in
pen Door Policy terms—puzzled Judy and me some,
specially when we were small. After the anatomical
rawings in the medical books had been displayed and
st precisely what part of whose anatomy went just
here fully explained, as it had been so many times
efore, my mother used to open the conference to the
oor.

"Have you done this with lots of men, Mommy?"
dy always asked that.

"Indeed not." That's what my mother always said.

"How many?"

"Only my two husbands, and only after we were
arried."

"What about Dexter?"

As I have said, the Open Door Policy was flexible in
atters of sentiment, and my mother would answer
ithout hesitation. "I was never married to Dex."

"His name is Dexter," I used to say to myself. "Not
ex. That's ugly. Dexter." Out loud I said, "What was

that other husband's name, then? I thought you wer
married to Dexter."

"No, no. I've always said Dex would be the husban
of my old age. No, no, not Dex. Sean Forsyth."

It never occurred to us that she would lie about
thing like that.

"I remember riding with Dex in Times Squar
once," my mother said, and you could hear the cares
in her voice, "oh, years and years ago, and makin
some conventional comment about how awful neo
lights are. He laughed and said, 'Oh, come on! I lov
them.' 'What for?' I asked. 'They're exciting,' he saic
laughing again. 'Just look at them. It's exciting just t
look at them.'" My mother shook her head fondly
"How can you help loving somebody like that?"

When I was eight and Judy eleven, my father wer
on sabbatical from the university; he took up a post a
economic adviser to Sir Stafford Cripps's governmer
in England, and the whole family went along. W
rented a house in Surrey with a huge stuffed turtl
hanging on the wall, coal-burning fireplaces fc
warmth, and a wood-burning stove that heated the wa
ter. Judy and I boarded at a private school i
Greyshott, where, because we were American—it wa
not long after the war—and Irish too, the other littl
girls peed in our bathwater. We said grace before an
after eating; each boarder supplied her own saccharin
and jam because rationing was still in effect, and w
called one of our teachers Miss Penis behind her back
Judy became anemic and I got boils. But what I re
member most about the trip is that we saw Dexter o
the way back through New York.

A few years afterward, when I was eleven, he cam
and stayed at our house for a while. My mother used t
send me to the guest room to wake him for breakfas
he slept without any nightclothes, his shoulders an
chest visible above the sheets, and he was usuall
asleep when I entered the room. My father was almos
woolly with hair; Dexter's skin was smooth and

uld see the muscles underneath it. He slept on his
ack with his head turned to one side, and the male
ace of his neck cast a light shadow on the pillow. I
ometimes watched, waiting, for as long as ten min-
tes before he woke.

In 1955 he published a novel, *The Accident*, and
avid Selznick optioned the movie rights; Dexter
ent to Hollywood to work on the script, and since we
ere not too far away, he came up to spend a couple of
ays with us. I hadn't known he was coming; I got
ome from ballet school to find a party well along. My
ather had gone to bed, as he often did; parties bored
im after dinner was over; it was the early morning
ours he loved, dawn and just before. There were
uite a number of people talking and drinking in the
arge living room.

Dexter sat alone in the room beyond—a sitting room
sed more for family occasions than for parties—with
drink in his hand. I watched him there, all alone at
he party in his honor, just as I had watched him sleep
our years before. I liked the way he used his hands,
hich were long-fingered and slender; I liked the way
e sat, knees apart, one foot atop the other; I liked his
ace, with its boyish contour and party flush and dark
yes; I liked the way his back reclined against the easy
hair, a little tensely, as though he weren't entirely
omfortable and could never be made so.

I wore my school uniform and he was melancholy.
My hands shook a little. I got out a dress I was making
or Judy, a blue taffeta affair I had designed for her to
wear to her senior prom, and I sewed on it while we
alked. Nobody interrupted. Dexter got up from the
hair and stood by the fireplace; there wasn't a fire
here, but I remember him standing in front of the
earth, one elbow resting on the mantelpiece. And I
emember that he stood, as he had sat, a little tensely.

After he returned to New York from Hollywood, his
novie unmade, he sent me a barrette with a blue
eramic design on it. It wasn't wearable—the ceramic

design would have come off—but I kept the barrette
a drawer and I looked at it from time to time. It lacke
the force of a talisman, but it brought that evening
mind if I concentrated hard enough, and I treasured
accordingly.

7

At the barre, *ronds de jambe en l'air* serve to loosen the ligaments of the knees just as *ronds de jambe à terre* served earlier to loosen the ligaments of the hip; abnormal suppleness in both joints is prerequisite to the sculptured distortions which account for the beauty of the balletic line.

DURING THE SUMMER VACATION, before the summer session at the ballet school began, Walt went with my family and me to spend a week at Fallen Leaf Lake, a charming small resort in wooded hills not far from Tahoe. One day, walking along a mountain path there among the ferns and pine trees, he and I managed to kiss each other on the mouth. Perhaps because we were both so well trained physically, the kiss had none of the fumbling usually inherent in a first experience of that sort—it was as much first for him as it was for me. The arms were comfortably entwined, the noses out of the way, the tilt of the heads in accord, a sense of something more than affection present. We were both delighted, and we walked down the mountainside holding hands. We held hands a good deal in the days that followed, but we never kissed again. Mostly we talked as we always had, always agreeing. And then one afternoon we disagreed. I took the gold ring on its gold chain off my neck and handed it back to him. He shook his head, his hands behind his back, tears rolling down his cheeks. I insisted, crying too. For almost a year and a half afterward we refused even to speak to each other.

The San Francisco Ballet School's summer sessions were busy and doubtless profitable. Prospective students applied from all over the state and from well beyond; massive auditions were held and each summer student placed according to ability. The vast majority of those who attended were close to beginners, given the standard of the school, although many had studied for years; most of the classes offered were elementary, and the advanced classes remained more or less the preserve of year-round students like Suki and myself.

That summer I found Miranda among the foreign influx. She hadn't changed much since I'd left Wanda Wenninger's; her soft blond curls encircled her face as prettily as they had before, and we greeted each other with much excitement. I asked what class she had been placed in.

"Something called Basic 3," she said.

"But that's impossible." I remembered, when I thought of her dancing, only charm: Miss Wanda's Dutch girl in pink toe shoes and a full blue skirt. And Miranda had studied seven years. Basic 3 was for third-year pupils, pupils on a level some three classes below my own. "They must have made a mistake, Miranda. Why don't you—"

"Oh, it doesn't matter, Joan. I'm just here for the fun of it. I don't care what class I take." I said she ought to insist on another audition; I told her I'd go to Harold myself. She laughed. "You'd better watch me in class before you commit yourself to anything."

So, under protest, I watched, and I was glad I had taken her advice. She was overweight; she was soft and weak and her legs were turned in. Her arms were tense; she had no elevation, natural or trained, and she had none of the cleanness of technique that marked even the less gifted of the San Francisco Ballet's regular students. Her feet flopped, her knees wobbled, her elbows drooped, her bottom stuck out.

She didn't seem much impressed with my not very well concealed worry about her. I told her I thought she ought to take classes in San Francisco all the time; I said, although I was by no means wholly sure, that she could remedy what was wrong if she took time to do it.

"Miss Wanda said you'd say that. Exactly that." She smiled and seemed pleased rather than the reverse. "But I don't want to dance with the San Francisco Ballet, so it doesn't matter really if I don't fit in here, does it? I'm going to New York; I want to dance for Balanchine." She cocked her head to one side. "Don't you want to dance for him? I mean, sometime later? In a few years or something?"

I told her I thought the New York City Ballet wasn't as good a company as Lew's; everybody in San Francisco said so. And then I told her that if I tried for New York, Lew wouldn't let me come back no matter how much I wanted to. She said she didn't understand why not, so I told her about the strawberry blonde who had been slated to become one of Lew's ballerinas; Suki had told me about it. She'd gone to New York, the strawberry blonde had, and joined Balanchine's corps. She'd wanted to come back then, but Lew wouldn't have her. She'd been—well, I didn't really know—sort of disloyal.

"That's silly, Joan. It's petty. Lew Christensen ought to be ashamed of himself."

"Well, she isn't all that good, anyway. Maybe that's the trouble, really."

The strawberry blonde took class once in a while when she was in San Francisco to visit her family; I'd watched her several times. She was strong—steady in slow work—and loose, things that, by comparison, none of us gifted ones at San Francisco were. But she

was—there was no mistaking it—somehow flamboyant. She danced with too much or perhaps too obvious
a sense of pleasure. She seemed to be just enjoying
herself, showing off a little, not taking it all seriously
enough. To me, she looked simply uncontrolled.

Miranda smiled gently. "It's just that she's expressive, Joan. Everybody here is so tense and grim.
You've forgotten what an expressive dancer is like,
that's all. Is she still in Balanchine's company?"

I admitted that she was, and Miranda smiled again. I
was puzzled that the strawberry blonde could execute
steps the San Francisco dancers found difficult, but I
didn't tell Miranda that. Nor did I tell her that the San
Francisco Ballet had received rather mixed notices at
Jacob's Pillow early in the summer. The Christensen
approach, one New York critic had said, was too aus-
tere to give pleasure to an audience, too restrained,
too much of a classroom approach.

None of what I did say seemed to do other than
confirm Miranda in what she already felt. All in all, she
said, she thought she would continue her training
along the lines Miss Wanda had set for her; she wanted
to acquire the New York technique, not the San Francisco technique. "And where can I get that better,
Joan, than with a pupil of Muriel Stuart's?"

I talked to Suki a little about her; Suki wasn't interested. "No talent," she said. "She'll never get anywhere. Forget her."

The fact is, most of the students, even those who
studied year round, could safely be forgotten. In my
class, for example, there were some forty to fifty students, almost all of whom were better equipped physically and better trained technically than students from
any other area of the country outside New York; of
these, perhaps as many as five or six were gifted
enough to be viewed as possible professional material.

Although the analogy has worn somewhat thin with
overuse, a dancer's body is indeed somewhat like a

musical instrument, a coordinated whole wrought from specialized ingredients, each of which must conform to an exacting standard: head, neck, slope of shoulder, curve of back, weight of bones, cast of pelvis, length of legs, shape of arms, hands, knees, calves, thighs and feet. The vast majority of the girls were healthy, athletic specimens; their drawbacks were minor ones, visible only to experts in the field, but sufficient to cut them off from a career in ballet. One or two of this majority lacked only a pleasing conformation around the hips or the requisite length of neck; about these the Christensen brothers probably reserved judgment. A spurt of growth, perhaps, or a sudden loss of weight, and the picture might change.

Clara Schaum was one who changed. She was a chubby little girl with a round face and a round behind when I first met her. It never occurred to me that she had talent; she looked thick-set and heavy-boned. But at thirteen she grew and lost some weight; her roundness gave way to an unexpected elegance of line. She turned well. She jumped well. She had a natural gaiety of expression I hadn't noticed before. She was in the class just below mine, and she was beginning to demonstrate for Harold.

The gaiety that marked her dancing had seemed, when she was still small and round, to mark her person too. She took the bus down to the train station after class with Suki and me and some other girls and took a train from there to an outlying suburb. She used to talk a lot and her humor ran to a brand of verbal slapstick that struck us, who viewed the world so seriously, as especially funny. But in the months after she'd grown and lost weight, she talked less; the slapstick, when she indulged in it, took on a hard and unfamiliar edge. Gradually she fell silent altogether, except for the occasional acid comment. She stared out the window of the bus, and, while we walked on to the train station, hung her head, preoccupied. "She used to take class

just for fun," Suki said, "and she's still trying to figure
out what's hit her. I'm sure it never occurred to her
before that she had even the remotest chance."

We had to walk the three blocks from bus stop to
train station quickly; the schedule was tight. We were
halfway along one night—there were six of us—when
we missed Clara; she stood some hundred yards behind at a street crossing. We called, but she didn't
seem to hear. We approached her and called her again;
still she didn't respond, but we could see her in the
twilight, head bowed, apparently in the preoccupation
we'd become familiar with, her schoolbooks scattered
on the curb and her hatbox dangling from her hand. It
wasn't until we were right next to her that we saw the
vomit pouring from her mouth. There was no noise, no
retching; it poured from her mouth into the gutter as
though she were a stone fountain in a city square.
When it stopped, her mouth stayed open.

"Are you all right, Clara?" I asked, reaching out
timidly for her shoulder.

She gave no sign of hearing me or feeling my touch;
one of the girls felt her forehead—it wasn't hot—and
she showed no awareness of that touch, either. Suki
studied her minuscule wristwatch restively. We
gathered up Clara's books, the girl who had felt her
forehead and I, and took hold of her hands. We pulled
her along the remaining block to the station; her legs
walked her there, if reluctantly, and her mouth gaped
open all the way.

We held a hurried conference, while Clara stood
silent, head still bowed, mouth still partially agape, off
to one side. Suki was rehearsing the next day; as it
was, she barely had time to make the train. One of the
girls said her parents wouldn't let her come to class
again if she was late. For another, the next train was
the last to her area. The others left for similar reasons.
I led Clara to one of the pewlike benches that adorned
the lower level of the station and sat her down there. I
found her telephone number in her school binder; her

mother agreed to come and pick her up in an hour. My mother was warm and reassuring when I called; she suggested I talk to Clara gently and find her a cup of hot chocolate somewhere.

I could not get Clara to say anything, but her face showed a slight flicker when I mentioned the hot chocolate. I took her by the hand, led her to a table in the station cafeteria, bought two cups of hot chocolate and put one in front of her.

She said nothing. After a moment or two she bent slowly over the cup and looked down into it; she studied what she saw there intently and her face twitched. "It's got skin on it," she said. Her voice was toneless and apathetic, but the words seemed somehow to bear the weight of revelation.

"I'll take it off," I said. "Let me have it." She shook her head very slightly. "Will you drink it if I get you some more?" She seemed to consider, and after a while she nodded. I went over to the counter; the waitress took the cup from me, stuck her finger into it, removed the skin and handed the cup back. I glanced nervously at Clara, but she was staring fixedly at her hands, which lay like a pair of cast-off gloves on the table in front of her. I returned with the cup. "There," I said. "It's all right now."

Again she bent slowly over the cup, more slowly than before, and again stared into it. "It's got skin on it," she said, and her voice was slower, duller, weightier than before.

She refused the third offering even more lethargically than she had the second; she seemed to be congealing in front of my eyes, and in some alarm I led her back to the station pews. We sat there in silence until her mother came.

Clara was gone for almost a year; somebody at the ballet school said she had been put into an institution somewhere. I found her sitting on a bench in the waiting room when I came to class one afternoon. I hardly recognized her; she was quite fat, round all over as she

had been once, and merry, lively, talkative, with, it
quickly appeared, a strong strain of slapstick in her
humor. She plainly remembered nothing about the
night with the chocolate; she couldn't remember much
about the weeks preceding that, either. She said she'd
been going to a hospital school, where she'd had a rest
and learned a lot. I asked her if she was going to come
back and take classes. She laughed gaily.

"Oh, no, not me," she said.

"But you were very good, Clara. You have talent."

"Look," she said, "it's just not worth it. I turn out to
be pretty smart—I never paid much attention to school
before, not really—and if I'm smart, what would I get
mixed up in that awful profession for? It's a killer."

As she spoke, she gestured at the back of a figure
heading for the stairs. I knew the woman well. She
took Advanced 1A occasionally; I thought her very
old, but I doubt, looking back on it, that she was more
than twenty. She kept her muscular legs, which bore
only the relationship of proximity to the rest of her,
swathed in heavy woolen tights; her cotton T-shirt revealed ribs visible in rows and held together, or so it
seemed, only by the skin that clung to them as though
vacuum-sealed. Lengths of bone joined her knobbed
shoulders to her knobbed elbows and her elbows to
her huge, gnarled hands. Her hair was black and
sparse, a Japanese beard, and the tendons in her neck
vibrated like cables in an open elevator shaft.

In most schools there is somebody who was once,
perhaps, in the company and has, unaware, grown ill
or old or incompetent, transmogrified from dancer to
gargoyle. I feared that anorexic, as the wedding guest
feared the ancient mariner; I never learned her name.
And I never saw Clara again.

I wasn't asked to understudy during the opera season that fall, but since *Aïda* wasn't being offered, I
wasn't too disappointed; nobody new was chosen to
understudy anything else, anyway. When the notices

went up for *Nutcracker* season, though, my name was on the list. I was to be an aquamarine flower in the "Waltz of the Flowers" in the second act and I needed to have a costume fitting. I had to go to the Social Security office in Oakland and get a Social Security card. Judy was jealous. I had to buy greasepaint, theatrical eyelashes, rouge, eye shadow, eyeliner. Alicia, the friend who had understudied *Aïda* with me, was an aquamarine flower too, and together we practiced putting on makeup; we spent hours in front of mirrors with elegant Japanese brushes.

The part was very simple; there were twenty-four flowers in six colors, and the aquamarine set was the easiest. I performed it with pleasure and without any troubles at all. We drove in buses, the company and such as Suki in one bus and the lesser apprentices like myself and smaller children in another; we gave performances in Sacramento and San Jose and San Diego and many other towns. There was a season at the War Memorial Opera House and a performance in the auditorium at the public high school in Berkeley. I wrote my autograph on the programs of small girls who waited in crowds around the stage door; I grew fond of the smell of greasepaint that lingers in dressing rooms; I received regular paychecks with deductions; and my classmates at school saw that I traveled with the company as Suki did.

8

In *serrés* one foot flutters rapidly about the ankle of the other; it's an odd, half-mesmerizing barre exercise that strengthens the sartorius—the long, handsome muscle that extends in a diagonal from crotch to knee—and the adductor muscles on the insides of the thighs, which a dancer needs for jumps with beats.

UP TO THE LEVEL of my class, Advanced 1A, girls were promoted in groups of a dozen or so; sometimes in the fall, entire classes were upgraded to make room for an influx of more elementary pupils. It was an elevated position within the school, Advanced 1A, but not without its hazards; promotions from it occurred only on an individual basis, and nobody but the gifted went into Advanced 2, the class the company took and the class Suki took.

I was promoted in the early spring. One evening during *pliés*, Harold suggested, in much the same casual manner he had used when he told me I was to dance in *Aïda,* that I try Advanced 2 for a few days to see if I liked it. All heads turned as I tiptoed away from the barre, and all heads turned as I tiptoed into Lew's class, which had, like Harold's, already begun. Nobody spoke to me either during the lesson or afterward while I dressed. Suki congratulated me later, on the

n, when we were alone; otherwise only the muffled
s of my erstwhile competitors in the dressing room
r both classes were over signaled that a change had
en place.

ew had a regular-featured, conventionally good-
king face and a model dancer's body; he carried
elf well, as most dancers do, and he had an in-
idating arrogance of manner. Most of us dreamed
ams about him and thought him exceedingly hand-
e. He was, after all, the head of the company, and
had, after all, been Balanchine's first American
llo. I thought he was a bad teacher.

is brother, Harold, taught patiently, working on
technical detail after another according to a line of
ument that remained consistent throughout the
rs. Lew changed his approach from week to week.
a while he emphasized strength, and for a while
ed; for a while looseness of the back, for a while
ckness of mind; but I could find no pattern in the
nges. What had been essential one week seemed to
ome trivial the next, sometimes to be reinstated a
nth later as though it were altogether novel, some-
es never to be mentioned again. I did not like his
sroom manners, either. Where Harold teased and
led, Lew ignored and insulted; where Harold en-
raged, Lew disparaged; where Harold was always
ised and often pleased, Lew was often angry and
ally disappointed.

a fact, I did not like Lew's attitude to the whole
of teaching. Harold seemed to demand work from
ipil for the pupil's sake alone, but Lew seemed to
iand it as a tribute to himself personally. There was
iething subtly degrading in paying that tribute;
iy members of Advanced 2 had difficulty maintain-
pride in what they did or deriving pleasure from
it they achieved. Technically the level of new en-
ts from Advanced 1A was often higher than that of
iy of the old residents of Advanced 2, and a num-
of the most promising students, eager and anxious

when leaving Harold's class, lost interest and ⌐
after several months of Lew's. It was perhaps so
recognition of his limitations that kept Lew fr⌐
teaching Advanced 2 all the time. Harold taugh⌐
sometimes, and Nancy Johnson—an interested and ⌐
ventive teacher as well as an exotic performer—tau⌐
it fairly frequently.

Advanced 2 was set off from the other classes in ⌐
pianists that served it as well as in the pupils who w⌐
admitted to it. For Advanced 1A and most of ⌐
classes preceding it, the pianist was Madame. Mada⌐
was the same diminutive Russian lady I'd first s⌐
some two and a half years before, and she still w⌐
fingerless lace gloves and brightly colored hats knit ⌐
in a 1920s cloche style; wisps of starkly dyed h⌐
stuck out here and there around her face like str⌐
twigs from a bird's nest. She had one of those s⌐
skinned Russian faces that age quickly, and while ⌐
was probably no more than fifty-five, the sag bene⌐
her pancake made her look closer to eighty; vermil⌐
lipstick oozed in multiple creases up toward her no⌐
Her stockings, like her clothes, were silk; she w⌐
patent-leather shoes with bows on them. From time ⌐
time she drank from a pint bottle that always ⌐
across the highest strings of the grand she played⌐
hiding place that caused trouble only occasiona⌐
since for the most part she confined her music to ⌐
middle region of the keyboard.

She was not a bad pianist, considering the terri⌐
boredom of playing for dancing classes, of having ⌐
cut up Chopin into phrases of four measures each ⌐
dry those out into sets of eight and sixteen—the b⌐
following each other with metronomic regulari⌐
She'd graduated from the Imperial Conservatory ⌐
Saint Petersburg, or so it was said, and sometin⌐
tears trickled down her cheeks as she played; so⌐
times, moved perhaps by the whiskey or perhaps ⌐
her memories, she launched into an unsuitable piec⌐

sic, something with range and depth, and we could
r the pint bottle jump and bounce across the
ngs. Nobody spoke to her harshly, and at such
es Harold spoke to her very gently indeed. Lew, it
med, could not bear to have her in the same room
h him.

o Advanced 2 called on the resources of the Uni-
sity of California Music School, which provided
w with young men who thought playing for ballet
cers sounded romantic. They didn't last long. It
k a week to break them in, to impress on them the
d for a steady beat counted out in even multiples of
r. The following week they came to realize they
ren't really playing music for dancers to dance to at
but only rhythms to accompany the specialized or-
of body building that makes and maintains
cers. By the third week they came to have the
ling that none of us would know the difference if
y abandoned the piano for the bongo drums. After
t they talked irritably about the pay, and after that
y left.

or our part, we were always glad to see a new one
ve and rarely sorry to see an old one go. The first
k, it was obvious from the young man's face that
thought himself involved in something glamorous,
t the something glamorous was us. Furthermore,
il Lew had approached the piano the first dozen
es or so to knock out the rhythm he wanted with his
, the new young man played things we didn't often
r—Bartók and Hindemith and Brahms and
avinsky—and he played with excitement and some-
es even with passion. It was fun. As the days went
though, we lost interest in him as he lost interest in
we listened to his music grow dull and lifeless until
faint sounds of Madame playing Chopin for Ad-
ced 1A in the studio beyond struck us as fresh and
rming.

ut one day there was Irving. Irving was an abnor-

mally tall young man, with legs so long that th
seemed to start, proportionally speaking, where
navel should have been. He had a small head, wh
he carried well forward on his shoulders, and althou
he couldn't have been much over twenty, he was
most totally bald; only the faintest fringe of blond h
at the far edge of his pate was visible. His hands w
enormous and hung down red and raw at his sides.
always brought a large stack of music with him into
studio, and he set it down, a pile on the piano itsel
larger pile on the floor beside him, before folding
legs under the body of the instrument. His feet, d
ing intervals between exercises, walked themsel
around behind the pedals and wandered off to the m
dle reaches under the grand, which had the appe
ance, as soon as he sat down to it, of a miniat
piano.

To Irving we were not glamorous; we were fa
creatures from a world beyond his ken, and he play
like a man possessed. His size gave him power, a
the sheer volume of an instrument played with s
force was a new experience for most of us. We all s
we would be sorry when he began to fade. But even
the end of the third week, when Lew interrupted I
ing's flying arpeggios to bang out a regular beat, Irv
listened respectfully and rephrased without, so
how, diminishing too greatly the essential quality
the music. By the middle of his second month, Irvin
respect for Lew, who was no musician, seemed to
turning into something like awe. The piles of mu
sheets he carried to class grew larger; he notated th
with a carpenter's pencil. He used to close his e
sometimes when he played, and sometimes his fa
took on a look of pleasure intense enough to embarr
a watcher. I remember him playing the Chorale fr
Beethoven's Ninth while he looked like that;
opened his eyes briefly when Lew knocked ou
rhythm on the piano case, then he blinked, bit his

sed his eyes again and played with renewed vigor
complete regularity, the expression on his face, if
thing, more intense than before.

le began to appear at the school when he didn't
e a class to play for. He had long talks with
lame, to whom he displayed a courtier's defer-
e, bent over almost double so that she, who would
erwise have had to address herself to his belt, could
into his face. It was during one of his conversa-
s with her, held in hushed tones, that I observed on
face the only smile I saw her smile in the four years
tudied in San Francisco. He talked to Lew
never he could waylay him, and he talked to
old; he showed them his annotated sheets of
ic, which neither of them understood, and early asked their advice.

ecause he lived in Berkeley, he sometimes drove
i and me home; he had a high voice with a girlish
ness to it and he questioned us intently, if very
ely, about ballet. He wanted to know what each
rcise was for and how it related to every other
rcise. He wanted to know which muscles were in-
ed and how each effect was achieved and how late
ncer could begin. He told us, when we tried to
ge the subject, that his professors at Berkeley
e not happy with him. He was no longer interested
usic theory, which had been his field; he was, in
, no longer interested in any music that could not
rranged to serve the needs of ballet.

ving had been playing for Advanced 2 almost six
ths when he disappeared. A new young man took
lace, and for once none of us was interested in the
lopment and decline of enthusiasm he repre-
ed. We wanted Irving. Lew only shrugged when
sked what had happened to him.

ne day I arrived early at the ballet school, and at
secretary's request, delivered a telephone message
arold, who was upstairs teaching Basic 1, the be-

ginners' class. As soon as I entered the studio I s
Irving. He stood, outfitted in bright blue tights,
middle man in a row of tiny girls in tunics, none
whose heads reached a height much above his kne
His legs, aside from their extraordinary length, had
shape whatever—no calf, no ankle, no thigh, and c
the merest hint of a knee—and his feet were small
round, like saucers. His neck stuck out of a wh
T-shirt, elongated, stretched-looking, as though h
been hanged, and his small, bald head wobbled so
what unsteadily atop it. There seemed to be a waln
or perhaps a wren's egg, beneath his blue tights at
junction of his legs, but no more. On his face, thou
he wore that expression of almost embarrassing p
sure, and as I watched, he grasped the barre, wh
was at least a foot too low for him, and bent him
down in a shaky *plié* to the accompaniment
Madame's Chopin.

During the Christmas season, Lew, like his me
Balanchine, liked to have the younger pupils from
school perform in his production of the *Nutcrac*
Some of the gifted children from the upper reache
the basic classes played in the party scene in Act O
and for Act Two Lew chose a dozen tiny beginn
dressed them all in red, and sheltered them bene
the voluminous skirts of an enormous Mother H
bard figure; on cue they ran out, one by one, more
more and more of them until the children in the a
ence screamed with delight. And still they came,
more. The little girls in red were easy to cast
difficult to control. As for Mother Hubbard, she w
dame in the tradition of British pantomime, a ma
drag, a comic capable of exaggerated and foolish g
tures; to make her tall enough, she usually had to
played by an actor-cum-acrobat on stilts.

That year Irving played the part. He needed
stilts; he looked funny just standing still, and he
hilarious the moment he moved, his small head w
bling beneath a short, fuzzy wig, his huge hands f

ping ineffectually at his skirts, and that inane look of pleasure on his face. He managed to shelter the little girls with less trouble than any dame before him. The little girls were, as Harold noted, his classmates and his friends; he knew how to talk to them.

That year I was sixteen, and I met Jim in the spring. Outside of Walt, I had had little interest in boys; my friend Emily, who lived up the street, brought Jim to see me. I don't remember why. Jim was eighteen. There was something fey about him, as there often is about boys that age; they look as though they startle easily, like hart or wildebeest, and their eyes seem large in their not fully fleshed-out faces. Jim was blond and blue-eyed, but he looked like a blond and blue-eyed Dexter, and it was plain he thought me delightful.

We went out to movies and folk music concerts together; we heard the great singer Odetta in one of the early performances of her career and we went occasionally to bars where jazz played and poets recited. When the weather was warm enough we waded in the gentle surf out beyond Golden Gate Park. We kissed in the backs of cars and on the fronts of porches, not quite so chastely as Walt and I had kissed; Jim was well versed and versatile in the skill. But despite the fact that once I looked into his eyes I could not draw my glance away again, we did little more than kiss. There were still two kinds of girls then, and I was the kind you were going to marry someday.

I went to dinner at Jim's house with his parents, and he came to dinner at my house with mine. He was not a person of great intellect, as it turned out, but he had a delicate way with people; he sensed the atmosphere of a room as soon as he entered it, and he could both analyze what he sensed and bring about changes if he felt changes were called for. His diplomacy was deft far beyond his years and always in keeping with a strange gentleness in his nature that made the death of even a small insect cause him pain. It was odd, given that quality in him, that he loved me in large part because I was a dancer and because I never gave up a single ballet class to spend time with him.

My father and I took a long walk along the beach one day, and he talked to me about Jim and about his own love for my mother. He understood my feelings, he said, especially because Jim was blond and blue-eyed. He told me that his first wife, a mathematician, and a good mathematician too, had had dark hair like his sister Hope, whom he loathed, and dark eyes like his sister Esther, his father's favorite. He was twenty-one and very ugly, he told me, and he'd never been to bed with anyone before. He hadn't expected it to be the revelation it was; he'd married before he'd given the matter another thought. It wasn't until after some months that he really noticed the dark hair and the dark eyes. He had made his young wife pregnant more or less against her will and insisted she go though with the birth; by the time the child arrived, a boy with dark hair and dark eyes, his wife's career had been dealt a serious blow and the marriage was in ruins.

He'd left her and gone to Washington, D.C., as an economic consultant, and he'd seen and slept with other women, but all of them had had dark eyes and dark hair. "I used to think," he said, "that the only thing I really wanted in life was to marry a blonde with blue eyes. When your mother came along I simply could not believe my luck. I still can't. Sometimes even now, in the middle of the night, I turn on the light and wake her up, just to see her, just to touch her hair and look into her eyes. She's a lovely woman, your mother. A lovely woman." And he smiled at me, stroked my blond hair—I had been bleaching it quite skillfully for more than a year—and ran his fingertips gently across the brows above my blue eyes.

9

A *developpé* consists of a slow unfolding of the leg, high above the dancer's own hip; it is a beautiful movement, difficult, elegant, during which the eerie beauty of ballet's physical distortions is revealed for the pleasure of performer and viewer alike.

SUKI JOINED THE COMPANY formally early that summer; she signed a contract and became a member of a union. She went on tour to some far-off place, where she and a number of others were photographed sitting on an elephant. I knew I wasn't good enough yet for the company, but that didn't make me any the less jealous. I used to sit on the train alone, staring out the windows as I had two years before and daydreaming. Mostly I dreamed that Suki had broken her leg. But even in the midst of my dream, I told myself that she was too careful to break a leg, and the realization made me somewhat tearful.

One day, a nondescript man in a seat nearby leaned over and handed me a folded piece of paper; the handwriting, which adhered rigidly to the blue lines, was irregular and labored. The writer had made several attempts to begin, crossed them out and started again:

"My dear young lady, life isn't—"

"My poor child, nothing can be so—"

He had settled on: "Dear Miss, nothing is so terrible as you are thinking right now. It isn't right for life to make a young lady so awfully unhappy. I am a stranger only, but I have suffered and because of that I can tell you that you are to be happy soon again. I salute you for your bravery to bear up with such fortitude." The note was signed, "A well-wisher."

I folded up the paper and hid it in my pocket; when I looked around the car again, the man was gone.

One of the things that disturbed me about the tour—other than the fact that I wasn't part of it—was Lew's choice of ballerina. Nancy Johnson was dancing as well as ever and so was Sally Bailey, a good solid technician if not a very exciting performer. I thought about what Miranda had said about the limitations of the San Francisco style, and I wondered why no general explanation had been given for the presence of Jocelyn Vollmar, a prominent soloist Lew had brought in from outside the company for the course of the tour. I'd watched her rehearse. She was old—over thirty—and she danced rather like the strawberry blonde who had gone to New York and joined Balanchine's corps. She didn't endow what she did with what I considered a due sense of gravity; her style was as carefree and easy as her technique was accomplished.

I discussed these things with Ann McCallum, a girl in Advanced 1A who had become my closest friend at the ballet school. Ann was tall; her face was heart-shaped and her hair black. Her eyes were black too—at least, I remember them that way—and she was one of those people, like Harold, who seemed always mildly amused even when she spoke seriously. She could quote the whole of Swinburne's "Garden of Proserpine" and she did so from time to time, when I asked her to, allowing her voice, which reflected her amusement, to play lightly with the words; the poem took on a curious but threatening vitality that way, as though the melancholy of the thought struggled openly to master the speaker. She thought my concern about Jocelyn Vollmar was funny.

"Ballet's all right for exercise," she used to say. "It's more fun than the broad jump, and I like it better than basketball. I'll lay you a bet I get a part in *Nutcracker* this year. I'll enjoy that. But I'm damned if I'll sour my soul over it the way you do. I want to write poems. I want to live. I want to have affairs." She thought a moment. "Russell said he thought I was capable of an affair. I've known him since I was six—he used to push me on the swings. Do you think I'm capable of an affair?"

"I don't know. Why not?" With the Open Door Policy at my back, I found her question dull. "What about Jocelyn? Why do they need her?"

Ann laughed. "Lew had to get somebody who could manage the big parts in all those fancy ballets he's rehearsing, didn't he?"

"What about Nancy? Or Sally?"

"Oh, come on, Joan. Lew choreographs his stuff so they can do it, you know that. But with the Balanchine ballets, well . . . Besides, I like watching Jocelyn. She doesn't look like she's kneeling at a holy shrine all the time. She's having fun. I like watching people having fun. Don't you?" I frowned and she laughed again. "The trouble with you, Joan, is that you've forgotten how to have fun. Or you never knew. There's a party at Russell's tonight. Come. I'll give you a lesson."

Russell was nineteen and, like Ann, he was dark, but where she was pure Celt in appearance, Russell had a good deal of southern France or northern Spain about him; his smile was slow and his skin was light olive. He was, I think, quite rich. He had his own apartment, two or three large, handsomely furnished, book-lined rooms in a good section of San Francisco, and he handled himself with the sophisticated air of an expensive private school background. He'd been a tennis prodigy too, at a time when the game belonged almost exclusively to the rich. Until he was eighteen, he'd played the amateur circuit to lavish praise and the high hopes of several prospective managers. But at eighteen he quit and entered San Francisco State to study history; he took ballet lessons for exercise. "I got bored," he said. "I suddenly go so bored I couldn't stand the sight of a racket. I still can't."

Athletes' bodies are sometimes not unlike dancers' bodies, and Russell was well put together. He lacked the requisite balletic distortions, of course, but despite his age there was still some flexibility in his ligaments, and since the technical standard for men was and is much lower than the standard for women—much, much lower (as a dancer I know put it recently, "All they do these days when they audition a man is feel if he's still warm")—it was entirely possible that a few years more might see him in the company. He rather liked the idea.

What had surprised him most when he started taking class was the amount of sheer strength he, an accomplished athlete, had yet to acquire. After more than a year, his thighs still trembled from strain before the barre was over. He told me once he thought ballet called for the brute force of football, the speed and economy of tennis, the control of gymnastics, and the same fierce egotism required for professional participation in any of these. "And that's not counting all the other things," he said. "You can play any game you want without a spine that flattens out. You don't need a pelvis that tilts forward or legs that rotate out from the hips and knees and ankles. You don't need an intuitive grasp of musical phrasing—an intuitive grasp of timing, yes, but you need that for ballet, anyway. And you don't have to look calm and happy all the time, either."

I went to a number of parties at Russell's apartment. Girls I never spoke to at the ballet school went too, and boys from San Francisco State; from time to time members of the company came as well. The talk had to do with politics and poetry and philosophy; we drank a lot. Sometimes I took Jim with me; most of his friends could not see what he saw in me, and I saw nothing in them. His best friend tolerated me and I returned the compliment, but otherwise Jim and I spent our time alone or with Russell, who liked us both.

With some prodding from Ann, I managed to enjoy myself too; I found I felt more at ease at Russell's than anywhere else. Neither the Open Door Policy nor the Christensen grip applied there, and it was there one evening that Jim, with the skill so typical of him, repaired the eighteen-month breach between Walt and me. Walt had started performing lead roles during the time we'd not been on speaking terms, and he told me, after we became friends again, that he found the strain far greater than he had ever expected. One day while he was rehearsing out on tour, he had wiped sweat from his face with a white towel, and the towel had come away tinged with blood. Several doctors, after several electroencephalograms, told him that capillaries just beneath the skin sometimes break under stress in nervous performers. Walt had literally sweated blood, and he was rather proud of it. He had a new girlfriend; he was also rather proud of her. She was a very talented girl from Colorado Springs who has just joined the company, and he told me, much delighted, that her mother and father were as impressed with his eminence in the company as his parents had been with the eminence of my professor father.

In midsummer my professor father emerged from the most degrading experience of his life, and he did not emerge unscarred. He had seemed happy after the Hawaiian trip; he and my mother got along well for months; he'd worked hard too, getting up, as he had before his suicide attempt, at five-thirty in the morning to prepare for his eight o'clock classes. It was during this period that he had talked to me of his love for my mother. But one morning he was too tired to get up at five-thirty; he stayed in bed until six. The next morning he didn't get up until six-thirty, and the next it was seven. He went to bed just as early as ever, but after a week he couldn't drag himself out of bed until nine, and then ten, and then eleven. After that he got up only to take a bath, which he filled with lukewarm water; he sat in it and wept, tears running down his unshaven cheeks onto his woolly chest.

He thought he had cancer. And the thought made him cry harder because, as he saw it, if the disease had progressed as far as it seemed to have, it was obviously incurable: he was dying just as he'd begun to come to life again. Doctors were called and examinations made; they ruled out cancer, but my father thought everybody was lying to spare him. A psychiatric consultation was arranged. My father wouldn't go. A psychiatrist came to the house. My father wouldn't see him. My mother sought advice from friends and relatives, and then undertook to file committal proceedings. Another ambulance came; attendants, equipped with a straitjacket they didn't need, took him away to Langley Porter, a psychiatric hospital in San Francisco, where he learned all over again, as he had in defying God as a boy, that he was one of those very few people for whom tyranny is worse than death.

The psychiatrists were thorough. They interviewed Judy and me several times and pronounced us to be normal children. They talked to my mother often and to my father hour upon hour. At their urging, Judy and I visited the ward. It was an ugly place, drab colors, poor light, iron bedsteads. My father slept in a room with four other men, one of whom took up a stance every morning by the only window and stood there, unmoving, throughout the day; his back was swayed from the constancy of the position. He'd been that way for ten years, my father said. The three others seemed unhappy but otherwise more or less normal.

As for my father, by the time I saw him first, he looked angry and wholly normal. He'd known as soon as the ambulance came that he'd been placed at the mercy of enemies; by the time he'd arrived at the hospital, an hour later, he'd renounced his odd schedule and endless bathing. He'd simply ruled them out as, at the age of eleven, he'd ruled out God. The old hatreds flared up in him and he fought, his weapons sharpened by his years as a lecturer and his prestige as an academic, and his ardor fanned by oppressors whose repertoire of dull, scatological answers debased even the least important of the questions that assailed him.

"There's nothing wrong with him, Mother," I said. We were standing in the parking lot just outside the hospital.

"You don't know what you're talking about."

"Oh, yes, I do. There's nothing wrong with him at all, and if I were him I'd hate your guts for what you did."

"Get out."

"He thought he was dying," I shouted, retreating across the macadam, "and you toss him in a loony bin for his fears. Who wouldn't hate for that?"

"I don't think you should have shouted at her," Jim said later. His face wore a worried look. He held my shoulders with his hands and shook me gently. "No, you shouldn't say things like that to her at all. Not for her sake. For yours." He shook me again, as gently as before. "She's one of those people—she's almost too strong for her own good. Don't smile. I mean it. She's not somebody to be crossed carelessly."

The psychiatrists discharged my father after six weeks; they found him a puzzling case, unresponsive to treatment, and yet—well, perhaps his symptoms had been somewhat exaggerated at committal. They suggested that he and my mother both undergo some sort of therapy. My father told them to go screw themselves. At home, for several months afterward, he

watched my mother as though he were a lion tamer
with a new animal in tow; my mother watched me in
much the same way.

While Suki was still on tour that summer, a representative of I. Magnin, the leading fashion department
store in San Francisco, had chosen me to model
leotards for them. When the company returned, Lew
choreographed a ballet to celebrate the hundredth anniversary of the crowning of Emperor Norton, a San
Francisco eccentric who had become the city's mas-
cot; I waltzed in that with a slender boy named Kent
Stowell, new to the company at the time; he plainly
thought waltzing with a mere apprentice was beneath
him, although I waltzed better than he did. I decided
he was stuck up and too weak, anyway, to come to
much; years later I saw him listed as artistic director of
the Hamburg Ballet. When fall came, I performed two
small parts in the ballet entertainment provided for the
Opera Ball, the fund-raising social event of the year,
given just before the season opened. When rehearsals
for the opera began, my name appeared on the list for
three operas, including *Aïda,* in both the temple scene
and the triumphal scene.

This time around I loved the opera; I learned my
parts and I was not afraid. I found out that our dressing
rooms were high up because dancers are low down in
the opera hierarchy; the greater the status, the closer
the dressing room to the stage. Ours were as far away
as possible. Musical directors of operas don't like
dancers for the simple reason that audiences do.

The San Francisco Opera, like most American opera
companies, ran on socialites' money, and a large proportion of the opera audience attended for social reasons alone. Their boredom was a palpable force beyond the footlights, even though like dutiful parents at
an end-of-term play they clapped politely when they
saw clapping was called for and tried not to fall asleep
when it wasn't. The only break for them in an evening

of hefty singers dying inexplicably in foreign languages
was provided by the shapely young men and women of
the ballet, who, in the eyes of the singers, simply
cavorted about on the stage for a few minutes in flashy
costumes and naked legs. The audience always
clapped boisterously afterward. Or tried to, at any
rate. The affronted conductor, on behalf of the affronted singers, used to lift his baton as soon as the last
dancer exited, and the orchestra would boom out the
opening phrases of the next scene fortissimo, until the
most persevering enthusiast had been silenced.

Each singing star had his or her own coach, and
there was a director for the stars as a group. Each
soloist had a coach, and there was a director for the
soloists in general. The chorus had several directors.
The ballet had Lew. The supers—usually students at
Berkeley or San Francisco State, who for a dollar carried a spear or wore rags in a crowd scene—had a
director or perhaps two or three. The stagehands had a
director; the children of the boys' choir had a director;
the costume department had directors; makeup had
directors; lighting had directors; the orchestra had its
conductor. There were stage directors and artistic directors and administrative directors. There were several coordinating directors in dark pin-stripe suits and
shiny shoes, and there must have been a director to
direct the coordinating directors too, as well as the
prompter, a thin German who kissed the ends of his
fingers with loud, smacking Italian sounds.

The coaches shouted in Italian and German and
French at their charges and at each other and at the
conductor; the singers sulked, refusing to speak English to the various stage directors, none of whom
spoke anything else. Lew shouted at us. The supers
wandered around, perpetually lost, perpetually
dressed in the wrong costumes for the scene that was
due to begin in less than five minutes. Armies of
stagehands shunted huge platforms back and forth.
Scenery rose, trembled, fell, broke and got replaced.

The singers flew into tantrums and refused to go on. The ancient sound system crackled and hissed in the hallways backstage. A hush. Then the first bars of the overture sounded, the curtain rose, and—miracle of miracles—an opera followed.

Renata Tebaldi sang *Aïda* that year, and my mother and father came to see the first performance. Tebaldi was perhaps the highest-paid soprano in the business then; her voice was a lovely one, "velvety, sweet, and intensely feminine," as Harold Schonberg, music critic of *The New York Times,* wrote a year or so later. But she was, by any standards, a big woman, tall and barrel-chested, with shoulders like hams, and she towered over the small, squat tenor cast opposite her. My father never did see me dance that night. He buried his face in his hands and fancied to himself an Aïda fairy-like and delicate, and his refusal to sit up properly so irritated my mother that she hardly saw me, either. But they probably couldn't have picked me out from the long line of priestesses, anyway, nor from the rather more secular dancers of the triumphal scene; we were all performing the same steps at the same time, we were well rehearsed, and the heavy, stylized makeup, the long costumes and black wigs we wore, served to obliterate any remaining personal quirks that might have set any one of us apart from the rest. The fact that I was part of such a spectacle with such an important soprano impressed both my parents, though, enough to create a momentary pause in the tense atmosphere of our house.

Even so, my mother didn't like the idea of the Los Angeles tour the opera took as soon as its San Francisco season closed, but my father said I could go, and she had no choice but to give in. I left school for two weeks, carrying my books on the sleeper train; we stayed at a hotel, we dancers, and drew sustenance pay as well as rehearsal pay. And when we got back, the lists for the *Nutcracker* were up. I had to my vast dēlight bagged the best of the "Waltz of the Flowers" roles; I was to be a yellow flower, the front-line yellow flower at that, and I was to be a snowflake too, at the end of the first act. I wouldn't have been given either part if I weren't slated for the company the following season. Suki said so, but I knew it anyway.

Grands battements are essentially high kicks, the last exercise at the barre, and though they must look effortless and light, by far the most strenuous; when there are many of them—as there often are—and when they are set to the pompous gaiety of a military march—as they usually are—the strain and the effort to hide it become almost unbearable.

MY MOTHER ALWAYS said afterward that we shouldn't have drunk in the year with cocoa; to this day I drink whiskey on New Year's Eve with a forced and dutiful abandon, still fearful of whatever spirits I offended that night. It was just Judy, my mother and I. My father was in bed by nine o'clock; his relationship with my mother had deteriorated during the Christmas season. From guarded monologues and long silences he had progressed to day-long rages and week-long sieges in his study, with all meals delivered to the door, breakfast, lunch and dinner. During these times he spoke to no one.

In early January the list for the newly formed company went up, and despite Suki's assurances, my own conviction, and the promise of my *Nutcracker* parts, I was not on it. About a week later, as I sat brooding in the waiting room, the school secretary, a small, round, warmhearted woman, tried to comfort me. "Don't be so upset, Joan," she said. "It hasn't anything to do with your dancing, you know. It's just that—well, you probably know, but—anyway, your mother called Lew—"

"But it must have to do with my dancing. What else could it be?"

"—and I sort of—well, I listened in. And she's worried about you, that's all." I looked at her stupidly. "She told him about your father—all that, you know—and she said she thought you shouldn't be put under too much strain—to wait and see, sort of, because—well, you *are* rather emotional." She hurried on. "You show it on your face when you're hurt or anything. And your hands! I mean, when you saw that company list—oh, dear!" She fidgeted with the papers in front of her.

"You mean," I said, hardly able to formulate the words, "you mean, if she'd never called I'd have been on that list?" The secretary nodded. "Lew was ready to take me?" She nodded again.

At home, I shouted and cried and screamed. "For Christ's sake, Mother, there's nothing overemotional about me, and you know it."

She shrugged her shoulders. "Look at yourself right now," she said. "Look at your face. Go on, look at it in the mirror. And look at your hands. Just take a look."

"You're trying to destroy me!"

"I'm doing what I think is best for you."

"You told them I'm nuts. That's what it came to. Nuts!"

"I did nothing of the sort. I told them you were overwrought. We all are. And you with all that performing, those late nights and rehearsals, all those school days missed. And what about Bob? That alone is as much as anybody can take. You aren't superhuman. I just told them, I wasn't sure any more pressure should be put on you. That's all."

It was then that I decided to do what Suki had indicated I should do the year before, and I found it far easier than I'd imagined. Within two weeks I'd trained my hands to lie still in my lap and my face to remain expressionless except when I laughed. The control, when I was sure I had achieved it, gave me an odd and somehow satisfying sensation, as though I had withdrawn a few feet from myself and, in the role of overseer, could monitor what I hadn't really been aware of doing before.

Ann didn't approve. "You were just beginning to look as if you had fun occasionally," she said. "You're turning yourself into a wooden Indian."

Jim didn't like it, either. He'd liked the way he could see things happening on my face, he said, and my telltale hands amused him. But he was the first one I used the technique on—officially speaking, that is. He'd begun to talk about getting married, and I didn't want to think about that. My feeling for him, when I thought about it, made me somewhat giddy, but I knew it wasn't going to last. Not for either of us. The previous fall he'd entered San Jose State; in the course of the summer he'd lost his position as male high school sweetheart, to become an anonymous freshman in a third-rate college. He'd brought home "The Love Song of J. Alfred Prufrock," and he'd been proud of my tentative explanations, but his own pride had been hurt. I was, after all, a girl, and two years younger than he, at that. And because I was proud of him, my pride was hurt as well. He showed me no more of his homework; to some degree his hurt pride and mine cemented the bond between us, but the discrepancy remained. I saw it more clearly than he and, fearing it, used my newly learned face and hands to hide the evidence from him. I did not have to do so for long.

On February 17 at ten in the morning—a sunny Sunday morning—Jim's best friend, the one who tolerated me because of Jim and whom I tolerated for the same reason, called me on the telephone. He'd never done so before and he sounded angry; at first I thought he was playing a joke in singularly bad taste. He had to say it several times before I understood. Jim had died during the night, while I was sleeping. He'd been dead twelve hours. A visiting Texan, unused to San Francisco hills, had hit Jim's car broadside, throwing him out the door and against a brick wall. Jim had assured the worried Texan that he was all right and then he had walked from the scene of the accident—because he did not feel all right, no matter what he said—to a hospital some miles away, where he had lain unexamined for twenty-four hours. He died on the operating table, the dorsal side of every organ in his body shredded from impact.

The funeral was held in a large local church; many people were there, but few I knew. The coffin lay on a dais, and measuring it against my memories, I knew it was too small for the body it contained.

In the days that followed, I slowed my steps whenever I crossed the street in the vague hope that some car might hit me too. I had tried to prepare myself for the slow separation I knew had to happen, and that very preparation made the suddenness of the separation I felt, the ferocity of it, far worse, as though I had myself been guilty, if only in prescience, of the lacerations and the internal bleeding and the pain.

For the first time in my life I didn't care what happened at the ballet school; I went through my classes there as mechanically as I went through my lessons at Anna Head's. "Why don't you cry, Joan?" Ann asked. "Surely you don't have to carry this expressionless thing so far. You can't be as cold as all that." She peered anxiously into my face, but the overseer in me, who had learned so quickly to monitor my face and hands, only drew away further and mourned silently, watching with hardened severity and a shade of newborn contempt. And then Ann died too.

About six weeks after Jim's funeral, a group of kids stood waiting for me in the ballet school when I entered. It was a strange gathering; sidelines of boys and girls I knew watched like official witnesses at an ex-

ecution while Nancy Johnson sat me down and told
me, as gently as she could, that Ann had been killed in
a red Volkswagen that morning. It was nobody's fault.
There had been no pain. My overseer registered shock
from somewhere across the room, but there was nothing for the boys and girls to see on my face. Ann's
funeral was held in San Francisco. The coffin was
open and she lay under glass like a specimen. To the
left of her, from a high and shaky plastic stand, hung a
display of white carnations in the shape of a heart
more than two feet across; through the center ran a
jagged strip of red roses ending in a huge cellophane
ribbon that reached, red bow and ties alike, almost to
the floor.

During the Easter vacation, my mother and Judy
and I went to visit my mother's parents in Kansas
City; we'd been there two days when the telegram
arrived saying my father had had a stroke. We flew
back. He lay in the hospital bed in Oakland, bruised
and bandaged around the head; he wept when he saw
us but he could not say a single word. Aphasia was the
official word for it, and they doubted he'd ever speak
properly again. There was brain damage, they said;
they didn't know just how much. The blood clot that
had cut off the oxygen from his brain had been massive; his bandages covered a trepan. "Trepanning's
one of the oldest of all surgical operations," an eager
young intern told us, gesturing animatedly as he
spoke, "just cutting a hole in the skull, really. You find
evidence of it on skeletons of ancient Babylonians and
of those most civilized people, the Greeks." But the
operation had not relieved the pressure. The young
intern did not know why. The right side of my father's
face drooped, saliva dribbled from the corner of his
mouth, and his eye was no more than a slit. His right
hand lay on the bed like a piece of pork, and his right
leg lay under the covers in the same condition.
When, after some weeks, the wound in his head

seemed to be healing, they moved him to a rehabilitation hospital, where he was fitted with a brace to support his useless leg and a wheelchair too, so the staff wouldn't have to pick him up if he fell. His useless right hand got caught in the spoked wheels of the chair; they fed him antibiotics to clear up the infection that followed and to control, they said, what appeared to be a minor postsurgical inflammation in his head. And they catheterized him to save the nursing staff the trouble of having to communicate with an aphasic.

The stones my father had developed in his barbiturate-injured kidneys disintegrated and blocked his catheter; convulsions of the bladder forced urine down alongside the tube. He tried to tell my mother when she visited, but only strange, unrelated words came out: "kettle," "God," "sleep." From time to time he bent over in what looked to her like a deep contraction of the gut and his body shook with what looked to her like pain and he cried out with what sounded to her like the cry of a man in hell. "The problem's psychological," the doctors said. My father waited in his wheelchair outside while my mother talked to the staff psychiatrist; she heard that agonized cry from the hallway. "He's miffed at being kept waiting," the psychiatrist said.

That very day my mother had him transferred, over the outraged protests of doctors and psychiatrist, to the university hospital in San Francisco. There it was discovered that the postsurgical infection had touched the dura, the tough, fibrous covering of the brain, that his kidneys, ureters, bladder and urethra were deeply inflamed, and that he had become, through overmedication, immune to all known antibiotics. For weeks he lay supine with tubes feeding liquids in and tubes taking liquids out; it was, they said, a matter of time only. There was no hope. His colleagues from the university were attentive; they asked my mother to dinner and their wives sent fruit pies to the house.

But my father didn't die. The doctors congratulated

themselves; they explained to my mother, though, that they could now estimate the extent of the damage. Grave, they said, very grave. My father's colleagues, hearing the news, fell off in their attentions. Dinner invitations grew rarer and finally ceased altogether; no more fruit pies appeared. My mother wasn't much surprised.

"They're not my friends, Joanie. My friends are in New York. Those are Bob's friends—if that's what you call friends. There's no point in wasting dinner and fruit pies on somebody who won't die on schedule and isn't any use to you alive. If he'd died at Easter they'd be long gone by now, anyway. We've only got Andy left. He's the only one."

Andy was Andreas Papandreou, the Greek politician and my father's prize student, who, on my father's recommendation, had entered the economics department at Berkeley to become his colleague and, later, his chairman. My father understood, and like my mother, he only smiled when she could no longer hide from him the desertion of his former friends and colleagues; he had never expected any more from them. But when she told him that Andy still stood firm, his face contorted as though he were going to cry—he cried a lot those days—and the left side of his face worked. Spittle flew from his mouth. But he spoke then the last sentence he ever spoke in his life. "I give him my heart," he said, and fell back on the bed exhausted.

After a few months more Andy, too, found other commitments pressing, and my mother came to invent telephone calls from him whenever my father seemed particularly low; she read out loud old letters from him as well, putting in new words, knowing my father couldn't read what was written there himself although he could recognize the signature, which he studied each time when she finished. "Andy, Andy, Andy," my father used to say in a soft voice, shaking his head and fingering the notepaper. It was the one name he could get out reliably.

I graduated from the Anna Head School in June, went to the ballet school throughout the summer, and entered the University of California at Berkeley that fall. I didn't like it much. There were eighty people in my English class and two thousand in philosophy, which was taught by an old bore. I had trouble getting from Berkeley to San Francisco too; the university wasn't nearly as accommodating as Anna Head's had been. Suki, who entered Cal when I did, had learned to drive during the summer; she acquired an MG, which she handled with authority and dash, looking as she sat in it like Stuart Little, the mouse who loved Margalo in E. B. White's book and set out to find her in his bright yellow automobile. But Suki's schedule and mine were different, and she couldn't often give me a lift.

The opera season began; I had been hoping and more than half expecting to be taken into the company for it, but I was not. The parts assigned me were no better and no more numerous than they had been the year before. On reading the rehearsal lists I remained as expressionless as ever; I used to cry in my room at night, though, muffling the sound for fear my mother might hear and tell Lew I was still emotional no matter how indifferent I appeared.

The season opened, and I asked leave from the university administration to go to Los Angeles on the company's tour. Permission was refused. Midterm examinations conflicted with the Los Angeles season; either I took the examinations, the university officials said, or I flunked out entirely. I consulted Suki, who, without any argument, had been given the leave I sought; she asked on my behalf, but to no avail. I was not, as she was, a formal member of the company; I had no union membership, as she did, to back me up; I no longer had a father on the faculty, as she did, to argue my case for me. In the end, since I insisted on going on the tour, they simply discharged me from the university. When it got through to my father that I was leaving my education to dance for a company I wasn't even a member of—despite a three-year apprenticeship—he grew very upset; my mother, much to my surprise, only shrugged and said it was, of course, my decision.

After the Los Angeles season, the *Nutcracker* lists went up, and to my horror, I was given exactly the same parts I had danced the year before. On the second day of rehearsals I broke my foot; the sound of the crack was loud enough to stop the pianist and the entire corps. X-rays revealed a fractured metatarsal. They also showed that instead of the wasp-waisted bones metatarsals should be, my metatarsals were tubby, enlarged throughout their length like elongated birthday balloons. Four years of wearing toe shoes far too small had paid off.

I spent the Christmas weeks in plaster. To pass the time, I taught myself to type and set myself up a course in philosophy. I read a little Sartre and Kierkegaard and Nietzsche and Schopenhauer. I didn't understand much, but the sense of despair was clear enough and it made me feel less lonely. I worked with my father too; every morning for as long as he could bear it, I tried to teach him to write.

He had grown strong enough and deft enough with the brace that supported his paralyzed leg to take walks around the neighborhood. My mother tried to get him to carry identification with him, but he liked to leave the house quietly—it was the one thing he could do on his own—and he never took papers with him. If she pinned his name inside his pocket, he removed it before he ventured out. She was afraid he might fall, find himself in a police station or a hospital, unable to tell anyone who he was; he couldn't say his name. It seemed at least possible that with application he might learn to write it.

I drew lines on large sheets of paper and guided his left hand with my right. He was timid and shaky at first, like any right-handed person using his left hand, but he made reasonable progress. He traced the lines, arcs, and circles I drew for him, and fairly quickly learned to draw series of them alongside the traced ones. I started on "Brady." He traced the *B*, and after a day or two, managed a series of *B*'s when he'd finished tracing. He did the same with the remaining four letters. I wrote "Brady." He traced it and reproduced it. We spent several days just doing that: tracing and reproducing "Brady."

Then one morning—he seemed particularly alert that morning—I asked him to write "Brady" all by himself. I put the pencil in his hand, and he bent over a clean sheet of paper. He frowned. Slowly, carefully, he began. After a few minutes, an odd, rounded stroke that dribbled aimlessly off to the right appeared on the paper. He looked down at it and then up at me; he seemed, looking down at it once more, a little puzzled, but pleased too. I shook my head, and we started again.

When I was ready to go back to the ballet school, after some two months of hard and concentrated work on the part of both of us, he could produce on his own only trembling lines that led nowhere and meant nothing. Even so, my mother was a long time giving up hope for his speech. Speech therapists came to the house. They showed my father pictures of Donald Duck and Bugs Bunny; they were all very young, just out of school, eager and full of enthusiasm. "Bunny," they'd say. "Come on now, Robert, try to say 'bunny.'" My mother attempted more practical things. "A cup of coffee," he'd repeat after her, taking the mug and smiling. But then one afternoon, unable to reach the toilet in time, he defecated in his pants, and in an agony of shame, the tears rolling down his cheeks, he tried to tell her what had happened. "A cup of coffee, a cup of coffee, a cup of coffee," was all he could get out, over and over and over again like a record caught in a groove.

The plaster cast was removed from my leg in January; I went back to the ballet school in February, but things there were not as they had been when I'd left. The members of the company—always excepting Walt and Suki—no longer greeted me when they saw me. They seemed to have forgotten who I was. The girls in Advanced 2 no longer suggested coffee, and had other things to do if I suggested it. Pupils from the lower classes no longer asked my advice on blisters and diets, and I found I had, in fact, only one friend.

I don't remember her name now; she was not a gifted girl, not really. She'd been good enough to get into Advanced 2, but she hadn't improved further; she was considered, for that reason, someone not to be seen with overmuch. She wore a jockstrap-like support under her leotard—no baby pants—and I'd often looked at her unfashionably clad body with distaste, wondering how she could bear to look like that. But she sought me out, not because she saw in me someone with whom she could share her unpopularity, but because, as one who knew, she hoped to cushion me a little from the sudden shock of mine.

"Go to New York, Joan," she said. "Something's happened for you here. I don't know what it is. You seemed all set. But it's over now. Go, if you've got the money. Get away from here."

Despite her advice, I spent more time at the ballet school than I had before; I had nothing else to do, no schoolwork to finish, no friends outside the one, and I found it difficult to spend too long a time in my father's company alone. I helped the secretary sometimes, filing and sorting, and one day she told me, more or less incidentally, that my mother had called several times the year before, and at least once had talked as long as an hour to Lew. "It was all the same, you know, sort of thing as—well, she hasn't called in a long time now." She paused and rearranged the papers in the file in front of her. "But it *is* strange, when you think about it, Joan—do you realize that all these awful things that have happened to you—I mean, do you realize you act as though you don't feel a thing? The whole time—as though nothing at all can reach you?"

I sighed. "Was I just about to get into the company again?"

"Oh, I don't know about that," she said. "Lew doesn't like to take unnecessary risks, you know. You can't blame him, really." She laughed nervously. "And you do seem a little accident prone, don't you think?"

It wasn't long after this that Ruby Asquith spoke to me. Ruby was Harold's wife, related somehow to the English Asquiths, a very tiny woman with dark hair and an exuberant manner; she always looked happy. She taught class from time to time when the company was away or Harold was sick. "Look, Joan," she said, echoing my friend, "there's nothing here for you anymore. Nothing. You must go. You have talent and you can dance somewhere else. Go to New York. Go to Balanchine. Or to Ballet Theatre. You'll be all right there, either place. But"—she paused a moment, bit her lip, and avoided my eyes as she spoke—"see if you can keep your mother out of it. Do you understand what I mean?"

At home I announced my plans to go to New York, and the announcement had an extraordinary effect. Within a month, my mother, my father and I—Judy was at college in the Midwest—were on a plane together. It had taken that long only because the arrangements necessary for a six-hour flight with a man in my father's condition took time; otherwise we'd have left before the week was out. "If you want to go to New York that badly," my mother had said, "then you must go. We'll all go. You're much too young to live on your own yet."

PART II

1

Grands battements end the barre; the dancers form groups according to an unspoken territorial code—most of the real talent is to be found in the first row of the first group—and the center work, for which the barre has served as preparation, is ready to begin.

THE PLANE LANDED at La Guardia in darkness; arc lights cast an orange glow on the runway, which shimmered under a wash of spring rain. Dexter was there to meet us. His hair was gray, I noticed with some surprise, but his bearing and manner were just as I remembered them. That uneasy amalgam of tenseness and buoyancy in him delighted me more than ever, a liquid amalgam with a high proportion of mercury present—or so I thought of it, drawing, schoolgirl-like, on the truncated science course I'd taken at Berkeley. I felt more alive just looking at him than I had in over a year, and he kissed me on the mouth.

Usually my mother arranged for my father to sit next to the driver of any car they rode in; it was easier for him to get his paralyzed side in and out of the front seat than the back. She put him in the back seat of Dexter's car with me, though, and took the front seat herself. I was puzzled. My father half lay beside me, exhausted, his head thrown back and his mouth open wide enough for me to see the ridges in his palate glow green under the neon of the street lights. It was too dark to see much of anything, and I was not interested in the city, anyway; I was afraid of it and what it held. I kept my eyes on Dexter instead, and I saw that my mother did the same. The bright lights of the East River Drive lit the curve of his cheek at quick, sharp intervals, as though willing to reveal it to me only stingily, a glimpse at a time, through the apertures of a revolving disk.

My mother, perhaps to reassure herself, as I would have liked to, that he was indeed solid and real, reached out and touched the back of his neck, inclining her head toward him as she did so. I couldn't hear what she was saying—she held her voice too low—but there was a huskiness in her laugh that wasn't familiar to me. On hearing it, I realized, with a sense of victory more than anything else, that she had, despite all her pious protestations, slept with Dexter, and probably over a long period too. I wasn't remotely jealous; doubtless the Open Door Policy, in making sex so dull, served me admirably in that hour of need. The affair had the feel of ancient history to it, of Greeks and Romans and scandals in textbooks; besides, I was pleased with the sophistication I showed in seeing what was in front of me. And I was not displeased, either, at catching my mother in such an important lie; she had always been rather fierce on the subject of lying.

"You did sleep with Dexter," I said to her later that night, when he'd left us and my father was in bed. We had a suite of rooms at the Beaux Arts Hotel on Forty-fourth Street, where she and my father were planning to live until they could find an apartment. I was booked into the Studio Club, a YWCA hostel on East Seventy-seventh; my stay there was to begin the following night.

My mother smiled easily, drawing on her cigarette. "What makes you say so?" she said.

"Oh, it's so obvious. The way you look at him. Your voice. The way you lean toward him. Everything. I don't see why you went to all that trouble to disguise it. All that Open Door stuff. How long?"

"Oh, only once."

"Look, Mother, I *saw* you tonight. It wasn't once. How long? No, don't say no. I'll ask him and you know he'll tell me. How many years?"

She studied me a minute. "Five," she said. I burst out laughing. She shrugged. "I knew you'd find out sooner or later—when you were old enough to understand."

"Were there any children? Do I have any brothers and sisters I don't know about?"

It was her turn to laugh. "No," she said. "Would you have liked a brother or another sister?" I nodded. "Why?"

"I'd like anything that's part Dexter's to be part mine."

The following morning I auditioned for Balanchine's School of American Ballet, the school that feeds the New York City Ballet. Dexter, aware of my nervousness and aware, too, that a trip alone across the huge, strange city would serve only to increase it, had offered to drive me there, and he did so, pointing out landmarks on the way. I don't remember the landmarks very well. I remember Central Park, though, the trees in flower and the people in summery clothes; the sun was shining.

The American School, on Broadway at Eighty-first Street, was even more elegant than the San Francisco Ballet's premises near Geary Street. I climbed a wide staircase; there were two secretaries: one a receptionist, who sat out in front, took my name and told me to wait a minute; and the second, a Russian with an accent, Eugenie Ouroussow, who had an office to herself and asked me questions, writing down my answers on a printed form. Mrs. Ouroussow wasn't much interested in my performing experience, or so it seemed; at any rate, I told her very little about it. I had been studying six years—that interested her—and I was in the San Francisco Ballet School's most advanced class—that interested her too, although not so much as my age, address and general state of health did. The interview was brief; she was a kindly woman, large, with heavy-lidded eyes, and she told me with a smile to get dressed.

"Who's going to do it?" I asked tensely.

Mrs. Ouroussow consulted the application form in front of her. "Miss Stuart," she said, looking up at me with another smile. "Don't be afraid. She's very nice."

"Miss Stuart?" I realized I had come to believe that no such person really existed outside Miranda's and Wanda Wenninger's imaginations. "Miss Muriel Stuart?"

Mrs. Ouroussow nodded and smiled once more.

I recognized her the moment I saw her, even though she was an unusually handsome woman and Miss Wanda had been so singularly unhandsome. Miss Stuart's hair was pulled into a bunch of curls at the nape of her neck just like Miss Wanda's; she wore a flowing circular skirt as Miss Wanda always had; she smiled at me as she entered the small studio I had been directed to, and her smile was the same artificially sweet smile I had known so well four years earlier.

"Good morning, dear," she said. "You're from San Francisco?" The way she used her mouth was Miss Wanda's, the pursing of her lips as she spoke, and the inflections of the voice were Miss Wanda's too. I was terrified, and I stood at the barre holding myself rigid in what, even at the time, I knew to be an exaggerated version of Harold pulling at the belt around his thin belly. "Oh, my dear," Miss Stuart said, "who taught you to stand like *that?*"

"Harold Christensen," I said, feeling traitorous, betrayed, and on the verge of tears.

"Well, don't do it anymore, dear," she said. "You must stand like this." She placed her right hand on the barre and her left beneath her delicately angled breast just as Miss Wanda had, tilted her head, and smiled at me the way Miss Wanda always did; she turned then to look at herself in the mirror and her smile deepened a little. She gazed at it—the smile, that is—just as Miss Wanda used to, adjusted her eyebrows ever so slightly into a more pleasing conformation and turned the perfected expression back on me. "You must pull up from your diaphragm, dear," she said. "It is from your diaphragm that you dance."

She shifted my body forward, adjusted my arms, helped me to open my rib cage. "That's better," she said, and then shook her head, muttering, "What a way to teach a *girl* to stand."

We went through the barre, not too unsuccessfully, I thought, although a number of times she altered my position from the hard-learned one I had brought with me from San Francisco. When the *grands battements* were over, she told me to do some pirouettes. I did as I had been taught, fast, sharp turns with the working foot placed low on the ankle.

"Oh, my dear," she said. "What a way to pirouette! When someone asks you to do a pirouette, dear, do it like this." She placed herself in front of the mirror, smiled Miss Wanda's smile into it once more, and turned slowly, with admirable control, her foot placed at her knee.

As we walked away from the audition, she said, "I think you'd probably better take the intermediate class. I'm just not sure . . ." She trailed off.

"If I have to take the intermediate class," I said, surprising myself with my own forcefulness, "I'd just as soon quit right now."

She turned, eyebrows lifted. "Really? Oh, well, if

you feel that way . . . As a matter of fact, I'm teaching C Class—the advanced class, dear—tomorrow. You could try it if you want to. Do you?"

"Yes."

"And then we could have another little talk after that. Is that all right?"

"Yes," I said, letting out my breath. She turned to go away. "Miss Stuart," I called after her. She turned back, swinging her skirt. "Do you remember Wanda Wenninger?"

"Who, dear?"

"Wanda Wenninger."

"A dancer?"

"A student of yours," I said, adding unsurely, "I think."

She frowned a delicate frown. "No, dear," she said, patting her curls in a gesture wholly Miss Wanda's. "I'm afraid I've never heard the name before. Till tomorrow, then?"

My mother said, "If you'd come through that audition without any trouble I'd be worried about you."

"Why? Why shouldn't I do well?"

"You're no performer, Joanie. You know that. It would mean you were just hard. I wouldn't want that, and neither would you. But you got what you wanted, didn't you?"

After class the next day, Miss Stuart said, "You got through that very well, I must say. Much better than I expected. Were you *very* nervous yesterday?" I nodded and she clucked. "Poor dear," she went on. "Anyway, I think you're right. C Class is the place for you. You are very quick." She smiled her artificial smile and swept away.

C Class, the class just below the professional class, was divided into two halves, one taught in the morning and one in the evening; there were about forty pupils per half, and I took the morning session, which, as it turned out, contained the larger proportion of gifted pupils. Since I did not wear my glasses to class, it took me some time to separate the more gifted ones from the less gifted, but I learned many things in the dressing room. I learned, for example, that nobody in New York wore baby pants; few wore anything by way of support, and there seemed to be no fashion guide on the matter. There seemed to be no fashion in leotards, either, or tights or hair arrangements. It was very strange. The girls were quite uninterested in proving they could stand up under the pain of blisters, and they wore lamb's wool in their toe shoes as though it were a perfectly natural thing to do; that was strange too. To be sure, we had three hour-and-a-half classes on pointe each week, and without the protection of lamb's wool we might well not have been able to manage them all. But such cowardly considerations would not have held in San Francisco. The relief was blissful; I bought my lamb's wool in bulk at discount drugstores.

In San Francisco, if my toe shoes slipped off my heels, I used rosin to hold them; the rosin caused large blisters to form. In New York I learned that water served just as well and caused no blisters, and water on the ribbons kept the tag ends from flapping. As for the ribbons themselves, I learned to tie them in the slight depression between the Achilles tendon and the tibialis posticus, where the knot caused no discomfort and was more easily hidden; in San Francisco I had tied my ribbons according to fashion on the Achilles itself, where the knot had hurt and bulged a little. At my first visit to Capezio, a rather officious young man told me I couldn't possibly wear such tiny toe shoes as I had asked for; after some argument he fitted me in a 4½A, and, compressing my foot across the arch with a quick, deft hand, suggested I order specially made shoes with a strengthened sole. His advice resulted in an immediate improvement in class; I became a devotee of everything New York and had my ears pierced.

The conversation in the dressing room concerned

diets and knitting patterns and constipation; a good
number of the girls were still in high school, which
they attended sporadically and partly through corre-
spondence courses, but nobody was in the least interested in schoolwork. If it was mentioned at all, it was
mentioned only as a necessary evil to be got through as
quickly as possible; the only thing of any importance
was ballet. I kept to myself and listened; within a week
it was clear to me that there was a central grouping of
gifted girls and hangers-on, and beyond them, just as
in San Francisco, lay the vast desert of others.

The gifted girls here were not, however, like the
gifted girls in San Francisco, most of whom went to
private schools and got good grades; these girls, with
one or two notable exceptions, were almost aggressively illiterate, and they took pains to appear as
stupid as possible. Those who had trouble concealing
their intelligence tended to keep their mouths shut,
and all of them concentrated on narrowing down the
range of their thoughts as far as they could. It was a
fashion dictated, as I found out later, by Balanchine
himself, although I doubt he was aware of his role in
the matter; he had said somewhere that dancers were
stupid and so the pupils at his school worked hard, like
devoted pupils anywhere, to don this strange trapping
of their chosen career.

Ordinarily I, too, would have devoted myself in the
interests of art to the pursuit of stupidity, but I had a
number of other things on my mind. I was, after all, in
New York and Dexter was there; it seemed to me,
looking at the matter dispassionately, that I should go
about losing my virginity as expeditiously as possible.
I had read somewhere that the loss of virginity was no
fun for anyone concerned—the Open Door Policy did
not cover this aspect of life in any depth—and I certainly didn't want to put any extra burdens on him
when the time came. I consulted my roommate at the
Studio Club, Alicia Slater, the lovely black-haired,
blue-eyed girl with whom I'd understudied *Aïda* in San

Francisco. She had come to New York more or less when I had, and we planned to get an apartment together as soon as our parents would let us.

The Studio Club, so its literature claimed, "catered for young women in the arts." But most of the girls were secretaries or in training to be secretaries; those of us actually taking lessons in ballet or singing or piano were forgiven our infringements of the rules, provided they were minor. Alicia and I enjoyed our position there despite the gray iron bedsteads and gray iron desks and gray iron chairs and despite the brick wall onto which our window looked; for twenty-seven dollars each a week we got our room, our breakfast, our dinner, and freedom from our parents. These facilities, we agreed, ought to simplify the loss of virginity somewhat, although no males, not even doctor males, were allowed on any floor above the second, where a large lounge with overstuffed chairs and plastic potted plants served as both barrier and meeting place.

After some consideration, Alicia and I settled on Rudy Harnsburger, a robust all-American from Peoria, Illinois; he was healthy, he was fond of me, he was reasonably good-looking, he was available. Rudy had been a student at the university at Berkeley, where he'd studied engineering on a naval scholarship; he had carried a sword in *Aïda* for a dollar one season and he used to drive me home afterward. Just before I left for New York, he went to Washington as an ensign; he had his own apartment too. I telephoned him and he suggested I come down for a weekend; I could spend the night, he said, in the Washington YWCA. He said he would arrange it.

Alicia and I decided I should wear black underwear and change into a white nightgown made of fine cotton with delicate embroidery around the neck; we packed my bag with care and discussed the difficulties of putting on makeup after the event without seeming to hog the bathroom. As to possible pain, Alicia pointed out that anybody who could put up with pointe classes in San Francisco was unlikely to have any trouble with that. I left on the Greyhound bus after class on Saturday.

Somewhat to my distress, it turned out that Rudy had been entirely serious about the room at the YWCA; I had difficulty persuading him that I didn't want to spend the night there.

"Well, where are you going to sleep, then? I've got only one bed here."

"With you," I said determinedly.

He was shocked. "With me?" I nodded. "You mean . . . ?" I nodded. "What do you want to do that with me for?"

I had not expected any resistance; I became timid and lowered my eyes. "Has it ever occurred to you I might be in love with you?"

He thought about this a little while. "Have you got all your teeth?" he asked suddenly.

"What's that got to do with it?"

"Well, our family has always had good teeth, and I wouldn't want my children to be any different."

"I'm not asking you to marry me," I said, alarmed. 'I just said—"

"Don't you want to be an ensign's wife? I think you'd fit in well with the wives I've met here. Your manners are very good. It's just that teeth—"

"No, no," I said. "I just want—" But I couldn't bring myself to say just what it was I wanted; I took his hand in mine and looked at him soulfully, praying he would get on with it without any further delay.

He frowned, shook his head, but, disengaging himself from me, dutifully began to take off his clothes; he wore shorts with stripes on them, like my father's. I hadn't thought young men wore such undergarments. He left them on, too, when he got into his ill-made bed, and so out of concern for his modesty I abandoned the idea of my embroidered nightgown and crawled in after him wearing my black slip. He tried a tentative embrace, but his heart was not in it, and he pulled himself away with a sigh.

"Do you really want to play like little animals?" he said.

"Well, if we got married we'd act just the same, wouldn't we?"

"It'd be different then."

"How?"

"Well, we'd be married, wouldn't we?"

I returned to the Studio Club the next day, but neither Alicia nor I could think of a suitable alternative candidate. I packed away my black underclothes, fine white nightgown and specially bought makeup box, for use, I hoped, in the very near future. I was not sure just how much time I had left for experiment.

2

The first center exercise is usually a *port de bras*, a slow, controlled, sinuous series of movements designed to perfect the carriage of the arms and torso while allowing a dancer a few minutes' grace to find her balance in the middle of the room.

IN SAN FRANCISCO the teachers were American; in New York, with the exception of Miss Stuart and one or two others, they were Russian. In San Francisco we called our teachers by their first names; in New York the women were "Madame" after the French fashion, and I don't remember addressing the men personally at all. In San Francisco most of the corrections were verbal. "Get your leg more in back of you." "Turn your foot out." "Press your shoulders down." In New York, the teachers taught for the most part silently and by touch; they pushed and prodded their students into position with sharp fingers and strong hands as Miss Stuart had pushed and prodded me at my audition. It was just as well, really; few of them spoke English well enough to manage complicated sentences. The men were especially poor in this respect, always excepting, of course, Balanchine himself, but it was several months before I laid eyes on him. Both Anatole

Oboukhoff and Pierre Vladimirov, on the other hand, taught classes every week on a regular schedule.

Oboukhoff's classes were fun to take. Ballet exercises can be composed in an infinite variety of ways, but Oboukhoff didn't vary his much; he so plainly enjoyed himself while he taught, though, that nobody minded the sameness. He was a small, bald man whose Mr. Magoo face looked very much at odds with his trim body and imperial bearing. It was the girls' legs he liked particularly. He used to pick out one girl, any girl provided she was pretty enough, and place his hand on her hip while she took an arabesque. When her leg was at its full height, he would draw his hand lovingly along the length of it until he reached the tip of her pointed toe. And then he would take a pose before the mirror, fingers barely touching the end of the girl's ballet shoe with a gesture not unlike God giving life to Adam in Michelangelo's painting, trim body drawn up until his spine arched ever so slightly, head thrown back; there he stood for as long as a minute or two, admiring himself and her in the mirror together. "Ahhh, goot," he would say, half under his breath, in what seemed to be an ecstasy of delight.

Vladimirov, on the other hand, was a short, dour, unhappy-looking man with the stocky build and chunky face of a Breton peasant; his nose was crumpled and he had the air of a fighter who had been too long in the ring. Where Oboukhoff varied his classes little, Vladimirov varied his not at all; they were the same every time he taught. He sat through them watching us in an abstracted way, never correcting, mumbling out in French, when we had finished one exercise, the directions for the next in the monotonic voice of a depressive. He taught Tuesdays and Thursdays, and most of us dreaded the boredom of those hours.

I remember him speaking directly to a student only once, and the student he spoke to was me. We were doing a rather trying jumping exercise, and I had stationed myself in the first group of pupils. I remember that he seemed to be looking at me throughout the exercise, but so far as I could tell, lacking my glasses, he watched me without interest; the defeated hunch of his shoulders remained as always, and he might well have been staring, as he often seemed to, at the wall beside me and not at me at all. When I had finished and the second group began, though, he pointed his stubby finger in my direction and said, "Again."

I was out of breath from the exercise and half stunned that a word of English had actually escaped him. "Me?" I said stupidly. "Now?"

I thought I could make out a look of irritation on his face. "Again," he said a little louder, and straightened his back into a command.

Somewhat irritated myself, I went through the exercise with the second group. "Again," the voice said behind me. I turned around, my mouth agape; my lungs burned and I was winded enough to see spots in front of my eyes. He shrugged, his body upright and proud. "Your group now. Again."

I began to drag myself spiritlessly through the exercise once more, but after the first eight bars of music I felt suddenly—abruptly—powerful, as though some miracle had intervened to make me fully rested; I danced with a verve I had never even guessed at. That phrase "second wind" actually meant something, and I looked at Vladimirov in delight when I had finished. He nodded. "Good dancer," he said with what seemed to be a slight smile. Then he turned away and the defeated hunch settled in once more over his shoulders like a London fog.

Some years later at a fancy cocktail party on the East Side of New York, way up high in one of those buildings where the windows go from floor to ceiling and display the city to you as though it were the furniture in a vast aquarium, I met Germaine Ogier, who had taken classes from Vladimirov in Paris in the 1930s before entering the Ballet Russe de Monte Carlo under

Colonel de Basil. She was a small, round woman; she wheezed a little as she spoke and picked at tufts on her chair with tiny ringed fingers.

At first she didn't tell me she'd been a dancer. She said, eyeing me somewhat pettishly, that in her experience slender people were more interested in money than in anything else, so she told me about her pretty cousin, who had never had to go on a diet and had worked as a broker in the Place de la République years and years before. That was a daring thing for a young woman alone in Paris in those days, Germaine told me, and her cousin had hung around with theater people too, advising them for free what to do with their pitiful rags and bones of money. Germaine had worshiped her cousin—she wore silk underwear and handmade shoes—and thought she was silly, all at the same time.

"How'd she get involved with the actors?" I asked.

"Ah," said Germaine, shrugging delicately, "I did that. Not actors, though. Ballet dancers." It was then that she and I discovered our acquaintances in common; we ate canapés together and talked until the last platter was clean and the other guests had all gone home.

"I met a man in Moscow once," she said, "an old man who had seen Vladimirov dance. Vladimirov had been a 'brave' dancer, he said. If someone else did a double tour finishing in fourth, Vladimirov did a triple, finishing on his knees or on one foot. He always did just that much more. But he wasn't dancing any longer when I got to Paris. He had the studio downstairs from Preobrajenska. Her classes were very technical, very concerned with basics; Vladimirov's were completely different—much more adult. They were hard but what the Russians call 'dancy.' And if you were a little tired or stiff or not wanting to take class when you went to him, you'd forget about it almost as soon as he entered the studio. He was wildly exciting as a teacher— wildly.

"He wasn't all that attractive to look at. He had a

broken nose, which he covered with a false one when he performed, and he was small. But my cousin, who was a great judge of such things, said he was very attractive to women. He did seem to have endless women. I heard that Felia's mother accused him of having an affair with Lifar, but that was ridiculous. If there ever was a man who was not interested in men, it was Vladimirov. But I simply can't imagine what happened to him. Obviously something, Joan, to make him what you knew. Age—which does terrible things—age and his life with Felia, which was very difficult. Her jealousy, his unfaithfulness, her mother's interference. But age—perhaps it was that."

It was Vladimirov's wife, Felia—Felia Doubrovska—who was the leading teacher at the School of American Ballet; when the students spoke among themselves, she alone was referred to as "Madame." Muriel Stuart was known as "old Muriel." Her artificial smile and pretentious mannerisms, which had, as a matter of fact, looked more natural on Wanda Wenninger, gave us the impression that her corrections were sometimes malicious. We probably misjudged her. Probably she was just one of those people whose gestures are a little out of phase with their thoughts, much as the English sound track for a foreign movie is out of phase with the actor's mouthings. At any rate, despite her many undeniable kindnesses, we did not trust her; few of us paid attention to what she said. But Madame we loved and we took her word as gospel.

It was some time before I got used to Doubrovska's appearance, though; she was not at all what I had been accustomed to in ballet teachers. Like the cloche-hatted pianist in San Francisco, whose contemporary she was, she had that ravaged look Russian women so often acquire before they are thirty, and like the pianist again, she wore her eccentric makeup injudiciously heavy. Her lipstick, like the pianist's, radiated outward from a bright red cupid's bow along the vertical wrinkles above her chin and beneath her nose. Thick mascara unloaded itself upward onto the soft area above her eyes. She plucked out her eyebrows entire and drew new ones, thin, black arches, so high above the natural position that, intermingling oddly with the creases in her forehead, they seemed to lead a life of their own. Her hair, dyed a deep brown, lay marcelled along the sides of her face as though painted there like the hair on china dolls of a hundred years ago, and she wore a round spot of rouge on each cheek.

Despite the excesses of her makeup, she dressed with restraint for class in a black leotard, a tulle skirt open at the front so she could demonstrate easily, and pink tights, which revealed her legs as soft and knobbly, but long and slender; she carried a large kerchief of some filmy, pastel-colored material in her hand or tucked into the waist of her skirt. She used to enter the studio a little late and make her way on tiptoe with quick, tiny steps across the vast floor space while we watched her fondly from our staked-out positions at the barre; she always smiled shyly, an apologetic tilt to her head on that long diagonal run from doorway to front of room, and her filmy kerchief floated out behind her like a gossamer pennant.

She was no longer strong; when she demonstrated for us, the positions she took were neither clean nor, in themselves, instructive, but no dancer could fail to be moved by the elegant carriage of her head and the airy grace of her arms. And what her own limbs lacked as demonstrative tools her gift as a mimic more than made up for. "You are holding shoulders like this," she would say to some large male dancer, planting her feet firmly on the floor in front of him and hunching herself into a gorilla. Even the dancer laughed. There was no mockery for mockery's sake, no ridicule, no self-indulgence, no artificiality, no malice whatever.

I met her at the bus stop one hot summer day; she was going across town to shop and I was returning to the Studio Club. "Is not good to wear sandals," she said, looking at my feet with disapproval. "Is not good for muscles. You wear socks tomorrow, eh? And, John"—she found the diphthong in my name difficult—"you should fix face. To be prettier, yes? Why you not fix face?"

I tried to explain while we paid our fares that I didn't like to wear makeup to class because it ran; halfway through my explanation, we sat down side by side, and I found myself unable to maintain my point before that bright red cupid's bow mouth and those two round spots of rouge.

"Tomorrow, John, you fix face. Mr. Balanchine, he likes pretty girls. To put on a little here—and here—so—is not much trouble." And then she smiled. "But I will not scold. We have whole bus ride together, and I have scolded enough. You always wear glasses, John?" she said, peering into my bespectacled face.

"Yes."

"But never in class. I never see them."

"I don't need them in class."

"Why you don't—what is word?" She squinted comically.

I laughed. "Squint," I said.

"Yes, that's it. Squint. Most times I can tell when girls wear glasses. But your face is clear. No squint." She giggled and squeezed my arm. "You keep your secret well, John. I won't tell. Is a secret between us now."

My cocktail party friend, Germaine Ogier, who had studied under Vladimirov in his Paris years, had known Doubrovska a little too, when Doubrovska was in her middle thirties. "Felia was never really in the de Basil company," she told me, "although she took classes regularly. She was a close friend of my cousin's, but she was never friendly to me. It's interesting that you liked her so much. At the time I knew her, people said she didn't like younger dancers. I wasn't in her class at all, of course, but everybody thought she hated Baronova and Toumanova even though her own body was very beautiful and she was lovely to watch. Until she took classes I thought I was turned out, but after I saw her I realized I didn't know anything about it. She was steady too, rock steady. It's a pity she was so tall.

"She married Vladimirov before they left Russia, and it was he who wanted her to dance again. She'd danced in Moscow and with Diaghilev and then she'd stopped. I don't know why. Anyway, one day we were told that she was coming into the company to do 'Bluebird.' The rehearsals didn't go very well, and the night of the first performance she arrived in a state of terror. She was waiting in the wings to go on, and she said to me, 'Germenka, I can't do it.' She spoke to me only because I was a friendlier face than most—because of my cousin, I guess. She didn't know many of the others in the company, and she was always distant even with the ones she knew. So I said, 'Why?' And she said, 'I'm dying of fright.'

"She had a gorgeous costume on—feathers and sequins—and her legs were so very beautiful and her feet—arched like this—so lovely, and she said, 'I won't be able to dance.'

"It was a disaster. She danced with Lichine, who kept muttering unpleasant things to her: she was too tall; she looked too old in the face; she'd been too long off the stage; it was too late for her. And it was true. He made it as hard as possible for her, and it was all true. Her mother was still ambitious for her, you see, and so was Pierre; Felia had been such a marvelous dancer once. The man I met in Moscow a few years ago—he'd seen her when he was a young man, and he said, 'Oh, all the young men were madly in love with her.' I asked him if he would like a picture of her—I had one at home—and he said, 'I would give my soul for a picture of Felia Doubrovska.' "

3

There is a basic fear in human beings of losing balance, doubtless related to the fear of falling, and so it is that pirouettes are a dancer's trick step, defying, as they do, the natural order of things; like all tricks, once mastered they give the performer an undeniable exhilaration, a sense of freedom from mundane things, a sheer, sensual joy in movement.

ONE FALL MORNING—the air had a freshness to it, a bite unfamiliar to a Californian like me—I saw Dexter far ahead of me on the street. I had been thinking about him, as I allowed myself to do from time to time, rationing out such periods of indulgence like gasoline coupons in a crisis, and at first I was sure the figure I saw was only a convenient stranger, transformed by the intensity of my imaginings into the object of them. But no, there he was; that was his walk and that was his hair and those were his clothes. Cream-colored pants, light-tan jacket and black T-shirt: nobody else dressed like that then, particularly in October. I ran after him and touched his shoulder. He was out to buy wineglasses to go with the roast beef and Yorkshire pudding his wife was cooking, for he did have a wife. Her name was Christina Malman, and she was a *New Yorker* artist.

I knew little about Christina. I had met her when I was eight and coming back from England through New

136

York; she was understandably more interested in Judy, who had some graphic talent, than in me, who was interested only in Dexter. My mother disliked her intensely and spoke of her slightingly, but she spoke that way of any of "Dexter's women," as she called them. One Christmas, Christina sent us one of her drawings, a portrait of her younger sister in puff sleeves, a delicate rendition; my mother threw it away. "For Christ's sake," she had said, "that woman makes me want to throw up. I'm tired of"—and her voice took on a mincing tone—"sensitive people. The 'we sensitive few.' To hell with them."

I rescued the picture from the garbage can and it lay in my bottom drawer for years; I packed it in preparation for the New York trip, and hung it in my room at the Studio Club. Christina was not well, I knew that, although I did not know precisely what was the matter with her; there had been hospitalizations and doctors and my mother pursed her lips angrily whenever the matter came up. As for my plans, they did not include Christina, but they did not necessarily exclude her, either. She was, after all, a part of Dexter.

I knew of a good glasswares store; Dexter bought six wineglasses there and took me to lunch. We went to the Palm, on Second Avenue at Forty-fifth Street. We drank dry martinis together, two of them, and we ate poached eggs on corned beef hash. I cannot remember a single subject we discussed, not a phrase he said, not a word that passed between us; I remember instead the sounds the knives and forks made, the feel of sawdust on the floor under my feet, the tinkle of ice, the donkey laugh of a man at a table nearby, and the cold touch of the glass in my hand. And each of these things seemed perfect to me.

At the School of American Ballet I took nine classes a week, the prescribed program for advanced students; three days a week I supplemented that with a class at Ballet Theatre. Ballet Theatre was in one of its

many eclipses then; there was a somewhat aimless air
about the studios, but the teachers there were excellent, odd and interesting, and the classes were small
and rather informal. It was pleasant to get away from
the pressures that bore in hard at Balanchine's school,
just to take class for the sake of taking it, to dance for
fun without paying heavy tribute to technique.

The first teacher I had there was Igor Youskevitch. I
don't remember whether his English was as poor as
Vladimirov's, but I had long admired that face in my
ballet books, those high and hollow cheekbones, deep,
dark eyes, and the severe Slavic delineation. Above
the waist he looked exactly like his pictures. Below it,
to my vast disappointment, he spread out into wide,
prominent, earth-mother hipbones, from which stringy
legs struck out downward with a mutual independence
that bordered on anarchy; when he stood with his feet
together, the gap between his thighs could easily have
accommodated a volume of the *Shorter Oxford English Dictionary*.

Germaine Ogier had known Youskevitch well, very
well, when she was a girl and studying with Preobrajenska, before she entered the de Basil company, even
before she began taking classes with Vladimirov. "He
was with a woman called Marina Guth," she said, "and
Marina—well, *I* didn't like her. He used to have to
partner her. She'd say, '*Kreutze! Kreutze!*'—Turn!
Turn!—and he would try, pushing as hard as he could
and going, 'Ugh, uh, urg, ohh,' to get her around twice
before they both gave out. And for years my cousin
had a joke about certain parts of his anatomy. I didn't
notice, really; I thought all ballet men were like that,
but my cousin said she couldn't watch class when he
was there because her eyes went automatically to
his— Well, it was only after all this giggling of hers that
I realized what a colossal amount of things were collected there. Anyway, he was unknown and starving
then, and without Marina Guth he couldn't have paid

for his classes at Preobrajenska's. I never did think he was very good; he had a peculiar-looking body, with those funny hips and all that . . . well, but Irina Baronova danced with him, and I know she thought he was marvelous."

The star attraction among the teachers at Ballet Theatre was the once great ballerina Alexandra Danilova. In time I got over my surprise at Doubrovska's appearance, but Danilova's never ceased to shock me, no matter how often I took her class. She had plainly had her face lifted more than once—she shared that ravaged Russian softness with Doubrovska—but it looked to me as though the liftings had refused to hold, as though the skin slumped back unexpectedly from time to time in the middle of the night, perhaps, and needed instant repair which, because of the inconvenience of the hour, it didn't get. Her makeup came from the same era as Doubrovska's, but the effect was wholly different. Doubrovska's gave her an air of innocent gaiety, like a puppet Columbine; Danilova's paint looked to me as though it had come out of a whorehouse. The effect may have been in large part the expression that played about her mouth and eyes; she had, I thought, a rapacious look, an exposed Dorian Gray sensuality so naked that it was painful to watch.

The garb she chose for class was entirely in keeping; she glittered like a Woolworth's Christmas tree ornament, in shiny gold high heels and a tiny skirt, half tutu, half mini, made from silver sequins. She dressed her famous legs, grown a little flabby and a little stocky, in open mesh stockings and her chest in a bright red stretch top which revealed a broad expanse of yellowed and crepe-skinned cleavage; around her waist she wore a wide black cummerbund fixed with a huge paste brooch. There were half a dozen rings on each hand and an equal number of bracelets on each wrist; her ears, too, sparkled, with elaborate paste

pendants that swung and tinkled faintly when she
walked, as she usually did, with the boastful swagger
of a sailor on leave.

Most of her corrections were aimed at the boys;
there were always more boys in her classes than in any
of the other classes I took in New York. They came
from everywhere to Danilova, and she ran her ringed
fingers down their arms to correct their placement and
stroked their thighs into proper positions, making a
low growling noise in her throat as she did so. She paid
almost no attention to the girls, and she noticed me, I
think, only because my legs faintly resembled her
own; at any rate, she watched me from time to time
with the guarded interest she bestowed on the occasional girl who seemed worth it to her. "You!" she
shouted at me from across the room one day. "You
have the beautiful legs, and you use them like an old
woman."

She was quite right too, and she spent some time
helping me to make my legs work more as her own still
did; the comment and the ensuing directions comprised the most valuable single correction I received in
all the years I spent in ballet.

Germaine hadn't liked Danilova very much. "I
thought her old and unapproachable," she said,
"whereas Irina Baronova was more my age—and
Toumanova too. Danilova's face looked old even
though she couldn't have been very old at the time. I
was told that that was because she had been fat. Like
me. I was thin then, though. Slender, anyway. Well,
everyone said Diaghilev could never make a mistake,
you see. There was one dancer, though, Natasha
Branitzka: he thought she would make a ballerina, and
she was always known as 'Diaghilev's mistake.' Anyway, when he took on Danilova, he said to her, 'You
know you're never going to do anything unless you get
thin.' So she went on a frightful diet, and practically
overnight the fat dropped off her. But it left her face
lined and creased. Makarova's face is the same sort—

the kind of face that's never pretty, and it ages so quickly. I saw her the day before she defected, before she was glamorized, and her face was very lined, very haggard, sort of stretched, even though she was fairly young at the time.

"But your description of Danilova is so terrible, Joan. She was elegant when I knew her, the only elegant ballerina. The others dressed desperately badly. They had no taste, and when they got money they would rush out and buy the most dreadful things. My cousin used to tear her hair over them. At chic dinner parties you could always pick out the dancers; they looked like gypsies. Whereas Shura Danilova looked like a Parisienne. Even in class she was elegant. She wore leg warmers over pink tights—she had this terrible bone, this bunion on both feet, very, very bad—and she always wore a black tunic, a plain black tunic, and a plain black thing in her hair. All the others had long hair, but hers was short, and she wore a lot of makeup. Skillful makeup.

"She was wildly taken with men—wildly. And men were taken with her. One day I was sitting with a friend of mine—a man, a dancer—when she came into class, and I said, 'I just can't see what's so marvelous about her.' He looked at me with contempt and said, 'You just don't understand anything, do you?' I can see now, looking back at it, how right he was. She had lots of wealthy men around her, all the time, and then there were men in the company too, whom she liked just for themselves even though they didn't have a cent. They just couldn't stay away. But she was discreet. Never vulgar. She did seem awfully vain, though, and I'm sure she would have done anything—anything—to keep young. I know she had her face lifted many times. She and Felia used to do it together."

William Dollar, well known once as a dancer and at the time as a choreographer, also taught at Ballet Theatre, and I remember him, as I remember Dou-

brovska, only with fondness. Germaine had never met
him. His face didn't resemble the face he had when he
was younger, the face to be found in pictures of him,
but I can no longer bring to mind just where the difference lay. He was very kind and very nervous, always
polite; his manner suggested the timid hesitation of
some gentle night animal caught out in the light of day.
He held his upper arms close to his chest as though
gripping a glove in each armpit, and his lower arms
cantilevered out from his elbows; his hands flapped
limply, erratically, ineffectually, and he gestured a
good deal with fingers that looked jointless. His pictures show him with the overblown legs of a weight
lifter, but he wore pants to teach in and, despite the
pictures, I thought of his legs as thin and delicate; he
handled them like a man who had suffered some minor
paralysis which left him with a shuffling gait and a
spastic looseness at the ankles. He carried his head
tilted at an impossible angle; it almost lay along his
shoulder, and I used to worry about him, fearing that
he might slip in the street when no one was looking.

During the time I took class with Dollar, he put on a
ballet of his own using a number of students from the
school, those who would have been in the company
had there been a Ballet Theatre company then, and a
couple of soloists left over from the company's previous incarnation. I knew the ballet a little and liked it;
he had taught it a few years before to the San Francisco Ballet, and I'd watched the rehearsals. Despite
the fact that I was from the School of American Ballet,
he chose me for one of the secondary solo roles. There
was competition between the administrations of the
two schools—at least, the Ballet Theatre administration felt competitive—and a student like me from
Balanchine's school was looked on with distrust; the
few of us who took class at both schools were never
included in the periodic projected fillings-out of a Ballet Theatre company, although we were on the whole
more proficient than those who were included. It may

have been that in the absence of a functioning Ballet Theatre, Dollar wanted to begin building a company of his own, and if that is what he wanted, he would not have been limited by sophomoric loyalties.

The performance of Dollar's ballet was held before an audience of semiprominent people. Alicia Slater came to watch me, and during the intermission, a representative from a model agency sighted her. In the weeks that followed, she gave up her classes at the School of American Ballet. She carried a huge portfolio of photographs here and there, gathering jobs; her talk had to do with lighting and advertising; she went out to dinner with a number of photographers; pictures of her began to appear in popular magazines. About this time her father came to town and took us to see *Look Homeward, Angel,* starring Anthony Perkins. We went out to dinner after the play; her father and I talked politely over the vichyssoise, but Alicia spoke only in monosyllables and only when pressed to speak. It was most unusual. Her mood held until we were in bed at the Studio Club that night and the light was out. Then she announced, "I'm going to marry a man like that."

"Like what?"

"Like Tony Perkins. Who looks just like that. I'm going to marry a man like that."

No more than two weeks afterward, she came back from a blind date arranged for her by some fellow model; it was very late at night. She'd had to be let in at the front door with a key—a serious offense—and she was not entirely sober.

She shook me until I woke. "I found him," she said, crowing with delight. "I found him and I'm going to marry him."

"Who?" I was still groggy. "What are you talking about?"

"Tony Perkins, you idiot. I found him and I'm going to marry him."

"You're going to marry Tony Perkins?"

"No, no, no. You are an idiot. Someone who looks just like him. Exactly. Only a little taller. Do you think that matters? But just like him otherwise. Can I borrow your Rudy Harnsburger nightgown? With the embroidery?"

"Now?"

"Tomorrow."

"What's his name?"

"Jules something. I can't remember. Where's the nightgown? I can't remember where you put it."

"In the drawer. Don't you even know his *name?*"

"It's Jules. I told you. Jules . . . well, Jules something. It begins with a *G*. Or an *F*."

"What does he do?"

"I don't know. What difference does it make? I'm going to marry him."

She didn't come in at all the next night. I didn't see her until I returned from class the following morning; she woke when I entered the room.

"Joanie," she said dreamily, "guess what."

"What?"

She sighed. "I'm a woman now."

"Do you know his name yet?"

"Um. Flaam. It's Belgian or Flemish or something." She eyed me triumphantly. "And he's a photographer. So there."

"Did you wear the nightgown?"

"Forgot to take it. It was in front of a fire, too. We drank champagne cocktails and there was even a bear rug."

"Nice?"

"I don't know. I don't remember, really. We're getting married on Friday. I hurt, sort of."

"Where?"

"Well, where do you think, stupid? I'm bleeding too. I suppose it's usual. . . ."

The doctor, winking at the nurse who accompanied

him to our room at the Studio Club, explained that Alicia's ailment was known in the trade as "honeymoonitis." He advised her to hold off the marriage until Monday. Which is just what she did.

Alicia's decisiveness had always impressed me. During the months we roomed together, she bought my clothes for me; it never took her more than ten minutes to select what I needed or, for that matter, what she needed. Her choice was as economical as it was quick, and her taste was always good. But her selection and rout of Jules Flaam dazzled me. I met him, and he did look like Anthony Perkins. He was exactly what she had set out to get. I decided her approach was worth some study; I registered at the library on Seventy-ninth Street and borrowed their copy of Dexter Masters's novel, *The Accident*.

I had not read the book before mainly because I did not think I would understand it; I was also a little worried that if I did understand it, I might not like it. I started reading it in the morning. I missed class; I read all through the day and through the night that followed. It's a fine, dark, brooding work, prescient and powerful, poetry to the ear and Lysol on the soul—a modern Hamlet, as my mother put it. It had been reviewed widely and well, although I didn't know that at the time; I didn't know it had gone into a dozen foreign editions, either, or that the State Department had denied David Selznick his application for an export license, thus effectively banning the movie version. The book seemed to have scared people in high places, and it scared me too. I had been aware of a healthy element of hero worship in my devotion to Dexter, but I had not seen the justice of the feeling before.

The telephone rang a long time. "Who is it?" said a female voice, somewhat indistinct and decidedly edgy.

"Joan. I . . . Is that Christina?"

"Yes."

"Is Dexter there?"

"Yes."

"Could I . . . I mean, well, I'd like to speak to him if I . . . Could I?"

"He's asleep." There was a rather long pause, and she hung up.

Christina died not long after that. My mother called me at the Studio Club and told me she had died in the morning; it was not, I gathered, unexpected, although she was only forty-seven. Had I been older or more experienced, I would have allowed the man to mourn his wife in peace; as it was, I took a taxi to his apartment without thinking at all. Christina's younger sister and brother were there, both of them solemn, strained, quiet, as was Dexter. I sat with them, solemn, strained, quiet myself. I don't know why I felt it my right to be there, but I did, and when the sister and brother left at midnight I stayed on. It occurred to me that Dexter probably hadn't had anything to eat all day; I asked him if there was anything I could get him. He plainly wasn't hungry, but he said he could eat some scrambled eggs.

I didn't know much about kitchens. Dexter's was large and it didn't look like my mother's at all; the high ceiling was dark gray, and some of Christina's *New Yorker* covers hung on the walls. My mother's kitchen was aseptic and hospital-colored. I didn't know much about cooking, either; I'd once cooked a package of frozen peas, but I couldn't remember just how I'd gone about it. I studied an old and tattered *Joy of Cooking* I found, and some twenty minutes later, sweating and trembling, delivered eggs in a more or less scrambled state. He ate and I watched, delighted and somewhat guilty too, knowing delight was out of place.

Dexter took Christina's body to Springfield, Illinois, where he was born; she lies buried not far from there in the very cemetery that served as location for the *Spoon River Anthology*. Like many schoolchildren, I'd learned about that graveyard. I could recite a line or two of Ann Rutledge, "Beloved of Abraham Lincoln . . ./Wedded to him, not through union,/But through separation," and I remembered something of the Purkapile marriage and Lucinda Matlock too, but I don't think I'd realized before—not really—that it was Dexter's uncle who'd written the poems, and it certainly never occurred to me that real people got buried in that cemetery. But that's where Dexter took Christina, and I know, because I asked him, that the graveyard stands on a hill and stretches down toward the Sangamon River below. There are old oak trees there, lots of them, and through them you see rolling countryside—"rolling countryside is unusual in Illinois," he told me. A path leads to Ann Rutledge's tombstone, on which the familiar poem is etched, and then takes a turning; a little off to one side, under a very large oak tree, stands a simple marble slab with these words on it:

CHRISTINA MALMAN MASTERS

December 2, 1911   January 14, 1959

Here's the rain, that's to wash you,
And the meadow roots to hold you tight,
Lie quiet, love.
Here's a robe of earth and a crown of dew,
For the shining face here's the mask of night
(And worms to circle the dancing feet
And a stone for where the wonder was)—
Lie quiet, sweet:
Here's the end of pain
And flowers to bring you back again.

Dexter wrote that. And when he returned to New York, drawn and sad and lonely, I was at his apartment to meet him, and I was there every evening for the next week. Then I decided with the delicate sense of timing people in love often feel they have—and sometimes do have—that the time had come. I packed my fine cotton nightgown with the embroidery around the neck and, garbed in it, carried out my plan with Dexter as ruthlessly as and rather more successfully, considering her honeymoonitis, than Alicia had carried out hers with Jules Flaam.

It was, I suppose, inevitable that my mother find out what I had done. I spent too much time with Dexter, who was to some degree shocked and shamed by the relationship and to a considerable degree guilt-ridden too. He tried to break away; he said the whole thing was wrong, and he said I shouldn't come to his apartment anymore. But his tone didn't carry complete conviction, and I was determined. Besides, I had decided he needed me, if only for my scrambled eggs.

My mother took me to lunch and leaned her elbows on the table. "If Dexter had a son," she said, "I would never betray him with the boy as he's betrayed me with you."

"Look, Mother, it was all my idea. You must know that. I pushed him into it. I had it all—"

"Nonsense, you're only a child."

"I don't think you know much about me at all."

"He's an old man, Joanie. Don't you see? He's over fifty. He's only fit for an old woman like me. You're wasting your youth on him."

"Who do *you* want me to waste my youth on?"

"Can't you find some boy your own age?"

"I want Dexter. Nobody else. He's all I want. Ever."

She shook her head. "It's wrong, Joanie. Wrong. And I'll do anything I can to stop it."

"Why don't you just refuse to pay for my ballet lessons?" I said maliciously.

She reached out and took my hand in hers, turning it over and back again, studying first the palm and then the back and then the palm again. She was, I thought, looking at her, tired beyond relief in sleep; she sat opposite me with her back slightly hunched as though the faith she had once had in humankind had suddenly died, leaving her honor-bound to carry its corpse to the grave on her shoulders, and the grimness of her mission combined with the weight of her burden gave a hard set to her jaw. She sighed, squeezed my hand, replaced it on the table, and looked up at me. I was suddenly—alarmingly—aware that the joke about Dexter being the husband of her old age was no joke after all. My father had always said he would die before his time, and he was proceeding, albeit slowly, to do just that; doubtless he had agreed with her that she should go back to Dexter after his death. She saw the alarm in my face and nodded. Then she pushed her chair away from the table and walked out of the restaurant without another word.

4

An adagio is a balancing act; the dancer stands on one leg and moves her arms and her other leg in serpentine, slow, patterned sweeps, tracing geometric forms in the air around her, arcs, chords, unexpected angles; a technical flaw so minor as poorly grouped fingers spoils the effect entirely, and the strength called for is very great.

NOT LONG AFTER Alicia got married, I sublet an apartment with another ballet student, Leah Penick, whom I had met at the Studio Club. We lived for several months on Ninth Avenue just across from the bus station; it was a noisy place, especially at six in the morning, when the buses roared out together to start the day, and a somewhat cramped place too, but it gave us more freedom than the Studio Club and we were delighted with it. We both had, as Leah put it, rather unorthodox private lives. She knew about Dexter and approved of my enterprise in the affair, but she remained secretive about her own comings and goings, which were, I noted, almost military in their regularity; she spent the same evenings out each week, and left the apartment and returned to it according to a never-varying schedule. She only smiled when I questioned her and said, rather shyly, that she would tell me all about it one day soon.

Leah had red hair, deep dark red hair the color of the earth west of Santa Fe, where she was born. She was exceptionally pretty. Like all serious pupils at the American School, where she took class every day, she was underweight, but her body had a voluptuous quality even so, a luxurious, almost profligate femininity at odds with the pared-down sleekness of the gifted pupils; it was enough to exclude her from their ranks, which, after I had studied there six months, plainly included me. But Leah's interests drew her more and more in the direction of jazz, and there was no ill feeling between us.

The gifted pupils in New York held themselves aloof from the rest much as the gifted pupils in San Francisco had. I first knew I was one of them when others of them began to greet me in the dressing room; they were not really friendly—I was regarded as something of an outsider—but they didn't shun me as I had been shunned in my last months at the Christensens' school and as they shunned those I could see for myself were not of their caliber. The exactness of my position was established fairly early: above Elaine, below Helen, alongside Rosemary. I knew this when Elaine, who had been busy soliciting Rosemary's friendship when I arrived, began to make overtures to me as well.

Simple observation and evaluation of students by students provided a partial basis for the positions reflected in dressing room society. The attention paid any pupil in class by the teachers was a much more powerful element, though, supplemented, as it was while I was there, by overheard snippets of gossip. Among themselves the teachers rarely discussed any but the gifted; sometimes the receptionist drank coffee with the teachers, and the receptionist's daughter, a talkative girl in the class just below mine, provided details which sifted down through whispered conversations to effect minor adjustments in the atmosphere.

The first few weeks I took class at the School of American Ballet, the top position in the hierarchy of gifted girls was occupied by a redhead, a pure henna-haired redhead, whose name I never knew. She spoke to no one and she cried in the dressing room sometimes after class. She was treated with the greatest respect.

"Why does she cry like that?" I asked one of the girls who had been studying at the school for several years. "She's obviously the best one around. She must be the next to go into the company, isn't she?"

"Oh, yes, she's next, all right."

"Well, what's she crying for, then?"

"The company's on tour. She wanted to go."

"So would a lot of people. I still don't see—"

"You haven't been here very long, have you? Well, look, she apprenticed to the company last fall and she made a hash of it."

"How?"

"I don't know. Forgot her part or never learned it or something. Anyway, she got left behind to sort of improve a little more. Mature, I guess."

"Maybe they won't take her after all. Maybe that's why she's crying."

"Don't be silly. She apprenticed. Mr. B. never drops an apprentice without giving her a chance in the company. Things can go wrong. He knows that."

I could not understand why the redhead had not learned her part, but I could get no more out of my informant than that "sometimes things go wrong." I tried to explain a little of the insecurities experienced by dancers on the edge of the San Francisco Ballet.

"Oh, it's nothing like that here," she said. "Mr. B. wouldn't act like that. Why should he? If he likes a girl, he likes her. He wouldn't choose her in the first place if he didn't. And if he does, why shouldn't he give her a fair chance?"

The company returned a few months later, and the redhead cheered up; within days of their return, she had signed her contract, and each of us in the hierarchy moved up a notch. The top position fell to a threesome, Carol Sumner, whom all of us thought the most promising and who is now, so far as I know, largely forgotten; Gloria Govrin, a tall and powerful girl who became a principal dancer fairly quickly after she entered the company; and Patricia McBride, who was considered a somewhat marginal case by the dressing room critics and who became one of the foremost ballerinas in America.

Carol Sumner's body was rather like Alicia Markova's, an ethereal, chaste slimness with long lines and the crisp, springtime elegance of a daffodil. She used to point at plump summer students and giggle with the fingers of one hand splayed over her mouth, like Yum-Yum in *The Mikado;* up close she smelled of stale sweat and nylon, but she was personally responsible for the lightness that distinguishes the American dancer from her European counterpart, and I shall pay her her due on that score shortly.

Gloria was more than five feet nine inches tall; she was not particularly elegant to look at—she had one of those overfeatured faces, like a Pekingese—but she was even then the strongest dancer I ever saw in or out of the New York City Ballet. There was nothing she could not do and do more times and faster and more forcefully than anyone else; she lacked only polish and age—I don't think she was yet sixteen—and I suspected her of being considerably smarter than she let on. Like Carol, she did her best to appear stupid, but she made sharp comments occasionally, and occasionally she seemed to have difficulty putting up with, much less matching, Carol's silliness.

Patricia McBride was something else altogether. During class she stood off by herself in a corner of the studio, near enough to the piano to feel its vibrations through the floor beneath her and close enough to the mirrors in front of her to fog them with her breath; she used to stare into the glass with a fixity that was unnerving, her brow slightly furrowed in the way of most nearsighted people. I remember her particularly bring-

ing her long, downy arms up over her head in the
adagio work, drawing them up slowly, languorously,
as though their passage through the air gave her ex-
quisite pleasure; her mouth used to open slightly and
her chin tilt up in anticipation of her hands' near meeting—an eventuality she delayed as long as possible,
bringing her fingers at last, almost reluctantly, into position, where they quivered a little, giving her the appearance of someone in the grip of a delicate and alien
ecstasy, as sensual and yet as innocent as a butterfly's
first stretch of its wings outside the chrysalis. To
watch was to trespass, but once people looked, they,
like Patty herself, found it difficult to look away despite the fact that, considered coldly, she wasn't handsome. Her knees were knobbly, her pelvis overwide,
her face bony, her arms and neck almost grotesquely
long. She had trouble keeping her legs straight too, and
she was always behind the music.

Outside class she was a shy, self-conscious girl, possessed of a childlike charm and a goose-girl simplicity.
She and Carol were best friends.

"Patty! Patty!" Carol said one morning, full of excitement. "I had the most marvelous dream. I dreamed
I got into the company and—"

"Oh, Carol, how lovely. Did I get in too?"

"Get in? Get in what? What are you talking about?"

"Into the company. In your dream. Did I get into the
company with you?"

"I don't know, Patty. What's that got to do with it? I
dreamed *I* got in and—"

"Oh, Carol, if *I'd* dreamed that, I'd have dreamed
you in the company too."

All three girls were in my class when I entered the
school; they were promoted into the professional class
a few months later, along with fifteen or twenty others.
The professional class was given at ten-thirty in the
morning, and it really was a class for professionals.
There were members of the New York City Ballet in it
every day. Melissa Hayden and Eddie Villella took it

regularly, Allegra Kent sometimes, Diana Adams and Eric Bruhn very occasionally; Jacques d'Amboise took it often and Violette Verdy, whom I'd first seen in San Francisco four years before, took it too, as did many of the lesser soloists. It was exciting just to breathe the air and exhilarating to become part of it (at least at first, before the novelty wore off), and yet the promotion was a very routine affair, not at all like my promotion into Advanced 2 at the San Francisco Ballet School. During a class the school secretary came into the studio and simply read out a list of names; all those who had spent two years as advanced students went— as I did the following year—into the professional class, and a contingent from the intermediate class took their places.

Patty, Carol and Gloria were, of course, also part of what was called the "Special Class," when it was set up to give especially gifted girls more individual attention. There were sixteen of us in the "Special Class," drawn from the intermediate, advanced and professional levels. We wore black leotards and pink tights, and Doubrovska taught us. Not long afterward, the three, along with almost half a dozen others, apprenticed to the company in *Serenade* or *Symphony in C.* I don't remember which. That left Rosemary Dunleavy, who eventually became the New York City Ballet's ballet mistress, and myself at the top of the hierarchy; but we knew, Rosemary and I, that it would take a long time for the company to absorb all those girls. In the meantime she and I danced in Gloria Contreras's ballets.

Gloria Contreras was Balanchine's choreographic protégée. She had shown him a ballet of hers some months before; he had expressed interest in her work generally.

"But what did he say about the ballet itself?" I asked her. It was a romantic, moody piece set to music in the style of a Rodrigo concerto and distinguished by full, sweeping arm movements and a delicate, feminine air.

She smiled wryly. "Well," she said, "he said to me, 'Look, Gloria, this is very pretty. This is like Gloria. But people don't go to the theater to see Gloria. They don't even care about her. They go to the theater to see themselves, and that is what you must show them.'"

With her small troupe of students, myself included, Gloria experimented with music of the electronic persuasion, to which she set semi-balletic contractions, sudden jerks of the head, and hands thrust out with the fingers splayed. The music was difficult to count and the movements unsatisfying to perform; Gloria pressed ahead grimly. Our rehearsals lasted as long as six hours at a stretch, held sometimes in an annex of Riverside Church, sometimes in a tattered, beer-reeking studio on Forty-fourth Street—wherever someone would rent her a room relatively cheaply.

She did not care for me as a dancer. "You have a beautiful body, Joan," she used to say, "but your eyes are dead. You have no personality. You're going to have to be satisfied with just being beautiful."

Ballet schools, like Mediterranean beaches, are filled with beautiful bodies. She might as well have said, "How nice that you have a Stradivarius. It's a pity you lack the talent to play it." But I had come to suspect on my own that I had no personality—none at all, not anywhere—and her comment filled me with dread; I thought about it until I came to think of almost nothing else. When I was with Dexter there seemed to be meaning in things, even in me, but without him I could find none. No matter how cleverly I probed and fished, all I saw inside myself was an ill-lit and shadowless interior, like an empty hospital ward at dawn on a misty morning—just what was indicated by that expressionless face and those expressionless hands I had so carefully cultivated in San Francisco. So I clung to Dexter all the harder; from being the object of my life he became virtually its only reality, and if it had not been for Carola Trier, I might well have quit ballet before the end of my first year at Balanchine's school.

Gloria took me to Carola's; I held my shoulders badly, and she said Carola could help me if anyone could. Carola worked from her apartment on Fifty-seventh Street, and on the wall above her desk, on which she kept her files, hung a small photograph of her as a young woman. She had been a vaudevillian in Germany in the 1930s; she had escaped before the Nazis came to power and her life after the escape had been hard in ways she only hinted at, but they had left deep creases on her face. The photograph showed her in her heyday as a contortionist on roller skates. In it she skated along effortlessly on one straight leg, her face as solemn as a bookkeeper's at a board meeting; I had to look at the picture several times before I figured out how the foot she wasn't standing on could have got to where it was. I decided she must have stuck her leg out behind her and somehow pushed it up until the thigh almost lined up back to back with her own shoulder blades. By some wild quirk of physique, she kept her spine upright while the knee of her upraised leg bent above her head, hatting her, so that her calf dangled down over her shoulder and her foot, heavy roller skate and all, jutted out—toe forward—from her chest.

In the bad years she abandoned her career and went to study under Joseph Pilates, a well-muscled man with an evangelical approach to body-building. Carola's technique included Pilates's exercises and work on spring-action machines designed by herself. She diagnosed her clients and prescribed for them, and she knew what she was doing. Dancers and businessmen alike went to her; she treated weak muscles, slipped disks and paralysis, all with vigor and an astonishing measure of success. It was she who restored a degree of function to Tanaquil LeClercq, Balanchine's ballerina wife who contracted polio, and she did so after the doctors had given up hope. Sono Osato and

Carmen de Lavallade, both of them past dancing professionally, appeared regularly at Carola's studio, but
so did Allegra Kent, who was at the time one of the
New York City Ballet's major ballerinas, and Nicholas
Magallanes and several others.

Carola listened attentively to what Gloria had to say
about me; I kept quiet. They poked and prodded and
discussed; Carola said she would think about the
difficulty I presented, and in the meantime, I was to
come three times a week for a half-hour session. The
sessions were terrifying. Carola was a small, tense
woman with a huge nose; she shouted and insulted,
her voice harsh and her manner cutting. Her comments provoked tears, and occasionally her clients ran
weeping from the room.

After three months or so, she called Gloria in for a
consultation; she had me in the middle of one of her
exercises, which involved taking a position not unlike
a swan dive.

"There, Gloria," she said. "You see? It's going to be
fine. What do you think of that?"

Gloria didn't say anything for a moment. "If *I* had a
body like that—" she began at last.

"But you don't," Carola snapped. "The trouble with
you is that you don't know how to bring her out.
Somebody will. And then they'll have something."

Her manner softened toward me after that; she told
me the little I know about her life, and she did what
she could to help me shake the doubts she sensed in
me. I came to look on her studio as a kind of oasis
within the dance world, a minor extension, almost, of
the oasis Dexter provided outside it, a place where it
was possible to believe, however fleetingly, that the
direction of things was not wholly aimless.

5

The first jumps of the class—very simply set—concentrate on developing what is known in the trade as *ballon*, that calm, easy, up-and-down bounce, which comes naturally to no one but which alone makes a jump look natural on stage.

NOT LONG AFTER Leah and I rented our apartment together, I got a telephone call from Walt Huron. He had been living in New York for several weeks, he said, and he would love a cup of coffee. "A cup of coffee," he said, "would be groovy."

He looked much as he had before and acted much as he had before; there was still somewhat the quality of a ten-year-old caught in a man's body about him, but there was something tense and forced too. He loved New York. It was groovy. He loved our apartment. It was groovy. Leah listened to him for a while and suggested we drink something stronger than coffee. Walt said that would be groovy. She brought out a bottle of Chilean burgundy; Walt went to the liquor store for another bottle half an hour later. The afternoon was warm and the windows were open; the sounds of Ninth Avenue had a summery distance to them by the time we started on the third bottle, and Leah could stand it no longer.

"What is all this 'groovy' stuff?" she said. "Don't you ever say anything else?"

"One adjective just doesn't seem your style, Walt," I said.

Walt smiled modestly. "I guess it's the company I keep." He looked at us through his eyelashes.

"And you didn't used to look at people through your eyelashes, either. What do you mean by the 'company' you 'keep'?"

"Can't you see there's something different about me?" I blushed; Leah giggled; Walt sighed. "His name is Rory Waterfall," he said.

"Oh, Walt," I said, "nobody could be named Rory Waterfall. That's ridiculous."

Walt drew himself up. "Well, that's his name. What's wrong with it? He's a painter, and he says I have the most beautiful body he's ever seen. He paints . . ."

"Yes?" Leah prompted.

"Sometimes, sometimes when we're—you know—in bed or something, he says—suddenly—'Hold it! Just like that! I've got to paint that.'" Walt smiled archly. "He's painted me dozens of times. Dozens."

"Do you like it?"

"Sure. It's groovy. There are pictures of me all over the walls, and in most of them—"

"No, no," Leah said. "I mean, do you like going to bed with a man?"

"Sure. It's groovy. It's the best way."

"How many girls have you been to bed with?" Leah had a direct approach I much admired. Walt looked a little unhappy; he hung his head and sipped at his wine. "Come on, Walt. How many?"

"None."

"But what about that girl from Colorado Springs?" I said. "You know, your girl friend in San Francisco. She certainly seemed willing."

"She wasn't, though," Walt said disconsolately.

"She wouldn't. Rory's the only one. I met him on tour."

"Why don't you look for another girl?" Leah said.

"I don't know any like that."

"Would you go to bed with me?"

Walt looked suddenly eager. "Sure, Leah," he said. "When? Now? Where?"

Leah laughed. "Ask Joan," she said.

Walt turned happily to me; I remember thinking that I could have made use of his enthusiasm some months earlier. "Don't be silly, Walt," I said. "Leah's teasing you."

"But Walt's serious," she said. "Look at his face. All hungry. Maybe you could find somebody at the ballet school for him, Joan. Or maybe somebody from one of my jazz classes—"

"Come to think of it, Walt, why haven't I seen you at the ballet school yourself?" He turned away from me abruptly, and I saw him close his eyes. "Where have you been taking class?"

He set his wineglass carefully on the table beside him and ran his hand over his face. "I'm through, Joan. I guess I just didn't fit in any more."

"Through? Not dancing? Why? You're the best dancer Lew's had since Conrad left." Walt shrugged, splayed out the fingers of both hands, and studied his palms. "Rory Waterfall?" I said as gently as I could. He nodded. "Oh, Walt . . ." He nodded again. "But why haven't you tried to get into a company here? What about Joffrey? Paula Tracy's gone there. And Mike Smuin too. Or Balanchine? What about him?"

There were tears in his eyes. "I'm just not good enough, Joan. A provincial company, yes; San Francisco, sure; but not here. Don't you see? If it weren't for Rory I'd be on the streets."

Leah and I remained morose after Walt left. We drank some more of the Chilean burgundy, mixing it with water to make it last longer. Finally, Leah said,

"I'm no better than he is. If it weren't for Leslie I'd be on the streets myself."

"Oh, come on, Leah," I said, "why do you say things like that?"

She shook her head. "I'm going to have to face it sooner or later, you know. Just like any other jazz dancer."

"You sound like a cheap novel. Isn't auditioning enough?"

"Sure," she said, "if you want to spend your life at the bottom of some crummy chorus. You just don't understand, Joan. I'm not dealing with your nice ballet world."

"Well, what has Leslie got to do with it? Is he on Broadway or something?"

She shook her head again. "It's just that with him around . . . I don't know. He half convinces me it isn't worth it. He's really more your type than mine," she said, cheering up a little. "He wrote a story in a magazine or a book or something. He showed it to me, but I don't know . . ." She looked at me speculatively and then grinned. "But he likes his girls with ample behinds. 'Leah,' he says, 'I like a generous behind on a female.' And you don't have any behind at all, Joan, so the match is off. Will you read his story? Maybe you can tell me what it's about. It's very grim."

I said, somewhat guardedly, that I'd be delighted to read the story, but I had decided I didn't much like this Leslie; the size of my behind was, I thought, rather agreeable. "Leah," I said, taking advantage of her mood, "why do you see him only on Mondays and Wednesdays?"

"Mondays, Wednesdays and Fridays."

"Well, why?"

"Because Tuesdays, Thursdays and Saturdays are Chip's days."

"Who's Chip?" Leah shrugged. "Who gets Sundays, then?"

"On Sundays Leslie rests. Like God." I laughed, and Leah shrugged again. "He says writers have to work regular hours and schedule regular hours for rest and relaxation. I'm rest and relaxation from eight to twelve Mondays, Wednesdays and Fridays." She watched me a moment and then started to laugh too. "He got a new desk last week," she said, "and he carried me from the bed out to it—he has an office, sort of. He was very serious, very grave. It was Wednesday, I think. We sanctified his desk to make it productive. That's what *he* said we did, anyway. Desks aren't very comfortable."

"Did Chip sanctify his desk on Thursday?"

"Probably. Or Tuesday. He couldn't decide whether to leave his manuscript on the desk or put it to one side."

"Good God, Leah, I hope you at least get a lot of pleasure out of it."

"No," she said, shaking her head and looking somewhat puzzled. "No, I don't. I don't really like it at all. That feeling coming over me—I hate that. I can't control it. I feel like I'm having a fit."

Several weeks later I came back from class to find Leah sick. She'd spent the day in the bathroom, she said, and bits of things were coming out of her still. We got the name of a gynecologist, but he wouldn't see Leah on an emergency basis unless we paid him first. Neither of us had enough money; it was outside banking hours, and so it was that I called Leslie. He seemed to dither.

"Look," I said, "she's got to have the money. Are you saying you won't help her out? After all, it's—"

"No, no," he said. "It's the doctor that worries me. I'm sure I know that name. What was it again?" I told him. "Yes," he said, "I'm sure. He's a quack."

"Are you or are you not—"

"I'll be up with the money in fifteen minutes, but"— he paused a moment—"will you go with her? I hate to

ask. I'd go but I don't think she'd like me to. In fact,"
he said sadly, "I imagine she probably doesn't want
much to do with me now."

Leslie was right; Leah took the money from his
hand and slammed the door without asking him in.
And he was right, too, about the doctor, who didn't
even examine her; he collected his fee and told her to
buy iron pills. The next morning I drew out enough
money from the bank to buy her a ticket home to New
Mexico. "Call Leslie," she said. "He'll pay you back."

Leslie appeared as promptly with the second pay-
ment as he had with the first. I suppose I'd expected
him to be pretentious in an arty way, a mustache, perhaps, and a pipe to go with shaggy hair and an oppor-
tunist's face; what greeted me at my door was a man-
nequin from a store window. The eyes were dark and
as expressionless as a baby doll's. The hair was dark
too, combed and combed and combed until it resembled an inexpensive toupee, and the body was upholstered rather than dressed in clothes that borrowed
their color scheme from a California family room or a
Holiday Inn; only the slightly protuberant buttocks,
hidden under the drape of a side-vent jacket, indicated
there was flesh and not horsehair under those soft-
weave materials.

His face moved very little as he spoke and the tenor
of his voice, which had sounded straightforward
enough on the telephone, was flattened out as though
he were reciting by rote. He seemed genuinely fond of
Leah, though, and genuinely concerned about her; he
urged me to call on him if I thought there was anything
he could do, financially or any other way, after she got
back to New York. He said again—and again, I
thought, rightly—that she probably wouldn't want to
see any more of him. We stood talking in the kitchenette longer than was polite, but his expressionless-
ness made me uneasy; I didn't want to prolong his
visit. He told me that Leah had talked about me a lot,
and that he found me, now that he'd met me, as inter-

esting, as intelligent, as attractive as she had said I was. "The fact is, I owe you quite a lot—for what you've done for Leah—and I want you to know that if there is ever anything I can do to repay you—ever—just let me know. Please." He smiled a waxen smile. "I know you've got yourself involved with somebody now, but if you ever get uninvolved, call me, will you? Anytime. Anytime at all." And then, with an upholsterer's touch to go with his upholstered body, he palpated my haunches swiftly and expertly, as though testing to see if the stuffing was correctly packed. "You know, I've always liked women with small behinds like yours, Joan," he said.

After he left I picked up the book Leah had given me and read his story; in it, the central character's father suffers a stroke like my father's and changes overnight, as my father had, from a man into a basket case. The violence of the emotion bore no relation whatever to the strange figure I'd spoken to in the kitchenette; parts of the story, full of rage, seemed to have been torn bodily from its author. It was the first statement I had seen of my feelings with regard to my own father's disintegration, and it came from the pen of an expressionless dressmaker's dummy—a person with, apparently, as little personality as I seemed to possess myself.

My mother liked to say she had arranged the move to New York because I wanted it, but it was also true that Dexter, who had just recently become the director of Consumers Union, had urged her to come to work there. She rented an apartment in Mount Vernon, where the organization's offices were located and where she continued her research into the byways of consumer economics, writing articles on what she found for *Consumer Reports*, the magazine Consumers Union published. The job paid reasonably well, and she was very good at it. She had become, in fact, a national expert on installment buying, credit, labeling, advertising, food additives, insurance; she testified on such matters before congressional committees and wrote speeches and testimony for, among others, Colston Warne, the president of the organization, to deliver. She had, I think, a genuine vocation, and her work was also her pleasure. It was her only source of relief, too, from the constant pressure of my father, whose demands, like those of all stroke victims, were practically limitless.

During July and August she rented a house on a small island off New Rochelle, not far from the Consumers Union offices and laboratories. It was an unpretentious place; the houses were simple summer cottages with chintz curtains beside windows that looked out over the water. My father was more comfortable there where the natural breezes kept him cool; heat gave him rashes that exacerbated the continual pain on his paralyzed side, and air conditioning gave him colds. It was there, during her brief summer vacation, that my mother began work on the final draft of *Organization, Automation and Society*,* the huge mass of unedited pages which was my father's last contribution to the field of economics; he'd been preparing them for the press when the stroke intervened. She sat at a folding table in the living room; he sat in an armchair beside her, watching soap operas on television while she worked. *The Edge of Night* and *A Brighter Day* flickered on the screen; she found she could simply ignore them as she ignored the sound of the surf outside. Occasionally my father picked up a page of his manuscript; he used to look at it with a puzzled expression on his face, shake his head as though in wonder, and shrug, his eyes already wandering back to the perils on the screen. He was happy.

My father's mother had been happy, too, when she had known she was dying. Her name was Margaret, Margaret Ginn, and she'd lived with the old man, my

---

*University of California Press, 1961.

father's father, for thirty years; she bore him seven
children, and she feared him every day of her married
life, from the first day until the day the doctors told her
she had inoperable cancer of the pancreas. She
stopped fearing him then. She couldn't understand
why her children took her illness so badly; she
couldn't understand why my father suffered so when
he saw her lying in bed, and she used to repeat to him,
a big, grown-up man by then, the verses she had told
him secretly when he was a little boy and they had
been afraid together. The old man didn't approve of
idle verses, but she was dying and she spoke them out
over the morphine in a clear, high voice.

> Once in the gone alow, was a biddy lum
> Sitting on a serb cone, chewing gubber rum.
> 'Long came a pig molicepan, said, "Willya gimme
>   some?"
> "Tinny on your ninpype," said the biddy lum.

In the euphoria that sometimes overtakes very seriously damaged stroke victims, my father forgave my
mother all those things he had held against her, and he
loved her once again with an intensity equaled only by
the love he'd felt for his own mother when he was a
child; if the television was off he watched her instead,
and he watched her like a young swain, with lingering
glances and misted eyes. Again and again he tried to
tell her how he loved her; he reached out and touched
her hair, but the words were wrong. Across the rickety
breakfast table in the summer cottage he clasped her
hand. "Biddy lum," he said, and shook his head furiously as he heard the words. He waited, formed his
mouth, practiced silently and tried again. "Margaret."
He shook his head even more furiously; he held my
mother's hand to his mouth and kissed it, then laid it
back on the table. His face contorted as it had when
he'd spoken his final sentence, and the word came out
soft, timid, rich. "Fuck," he said, and began to cry.

6

The teacher uses the small jumps—sliding steps, quick beating steps, intricate weight changes, dozens of them, all named and ordered like items in a Christmas catalogue—to create miniature eight-bar dances, which the dancer must grasp immediately and repeat right, left, right, left, without pause, knowing that the slightest slip of foot or thought will leave her hopelessly behind.

ENTERING THE NEW YORK CITY BALLET from the school represents the culmination of anywhere from seven to twelve years of hard labor; there is an almost inevitable tendency to relax once the contract is officially signed. A good proportion of dancers—a majority, in fact—stop going to class regularly and, like diabetics who lose interest in their diet sheets, begin to deteriorate. Technique grows sloppy and muscles weaken; injuries become commonplace and prospects of promotion within the company dwindle. A surprising number of dancers last no more than a year.

Among the females, marriage and pregnancy account for a considerable number of dropouts; a constantly tired wife who eats only yogurt and hard-boiled eggs doesn't contribute much to marital bliss, and it is difficult at best to get muscle tone back after childbearing. Even with these hurdles met, finding someone to look after a baby during rehearsals and the unhospitable hours of performances is practically impossible. Both Allegra Kent and Melissa Hayden had babies while I was a student at the American School; each took class until a couple of weeks before the birth, each was back in class a couple of weeks afterward, and each continued performing with only the most minimal of leaves. But both were highly motivated people, and both were, at the time of their pregnancies, paid well above the average dancer's wage.

Furthermore, there is a single-mindedness about ballet analogous to the single-mindedness of sport, and boredom is perhaps the most important element in the disillusionment of dancers, just as it is, according to the great racing driver Niki Lauda, in the disillusionment of athletes. The cocoon of firm paternalism and rigid convention that nurtured the adolescent becomes, as it does for all winged insects, a smothering encasement for many an adult dancer, for whom the passive charm of being a beautiful physical specimen is not enough to compensate for the color and excitement of the world outside. The make-believe, the dressing up, the lights—even applause from an audience and the approval of a man as great as Balanchine—turn into a child's trinkets, stylized imitations at best. Many dancers simply walk out one day, unwilling or unable to play pretend any longer. Some leave to go to academic schools; the Columbia University School of General Studies, for example, has probably housed at least one exile from the New York City Ballet every year since the company was founded. Others decide to look for jobs that are less taxing physically, better paid, and more befitting the personal dignity of an adult. Finally, a number leave each year to join companies where their names will, they hope, shine more brightly, and where the repertoire will give them, they hope, a taste of something different.

For all these reasons—and doubtless a good many others—there is a steady attrition within the corps and among the soloists of the New York City Ballet; the need for new dancers is constant. During the two years I spent in the American School, the company must have absorbed well over a dozen females and at least half a dozen males. Most were from the school, and of those, all—save one—were from the recognized ranks of the gifted pupils. The one, a girl named Beth, came as a shock to everybody.

When Beth first appeared, she was placed in the advanced class, C Class, though it was plainly somewhat above her level. She was a reasonably pretty girl; she had been well and expensively trained too—her daddy, she said, gave her whatever she asked for—but she did not have a ballet dancer's body. If any of us had bothered to assess her talents—which we didn't—we would probably have said she might at best, and with considerable effort, make the ballet corps at Radio City Music Hall. In any case, she interested neither the teachers nor the pupils who took class with her. And so it was with something akin to horror that we, the gifted ones, received the whispered news that someone had seen her in the studio when a company rehearsal was going on. We rushed to the door and, one by one, squeezed in to take a look.

Beth was not just standing in the room; she was dancing. From what we could make out, she was placed well toward the back of the corps, and it puzzled us to see that the part she was taking had apparently been altered to keep her there. But the blow was severe; we were scared. Those who had been apprenticed before Beth's arrival knew—it had always been so—that only the most extraordinary gift in another pupil would interrupt their orderly progress into the company; Beth was largely without talent, and the foundations of their world trembled. Those of us not yet apprenticed wondered nervously if some new plan of accession had been instituted; if perhaps Balanchine had lost hold or even if perhaps Beth's daddy had taken hold; if the company itself was doomed. A deep depression settled in on the school. The receptionist's daughter reported one unsatisfying rumor after another, until even Carol Sumner took to making remarks cynical enough to belie the silliness she'd cultivated so tenderly and well.

But Beth lasted only a season. Just one. Not even the contract year. And although she swaggered when she passed us, her former classmates, in the hallways, she danced the entirety of that single season where we had seen her rehearsing for it, in the farthest reaches of the corps, performing only in parts apparently modified to accommodate her inadequate technique. Then she was gone. I never saw her again, not in class, not in another company, not anywhere at all. Slowly the depression lifted. Something, we felt, had been put to the test, and the defenses had held; during the year that followed, all of the apprenticed girls, one by one, signed their contracts and entered the company. At the same time, several dancers from other companies joined the New York City Ballet. I remember a French dancer, who worked with Gloria Contreras while waiting for an opening, and Mimi Paul, whom Balanchine had seen dancing in Washington, D.C.; most of all, though, I remember Suki Schorer.

Suki was simply there one day; I had not seen her in the dressing room before class. She stood at the barre in what looked to me like the very same blue leotard she had worn on the first day I'd seen her in San Francisco, and she was as delicate as ever, too, as much as ever like a porcelain doll; the blue veins still showed at her temples. We must have greeted each other; we must have kissed each other on either cheek as ballet fashion dictated; we must have enthused a bit. But I was not glad to see her. For all that I owed her from my days in San Francisco, no sense of debt grew in me; she reeked to me of growing pains and old jealousies.

"Look at her," I said through my teeth to a fellow student. "She strains at the neck. She jerks when she jumps. She wiggles her fingers and ducks her head in a funny way. She's always done that."

My friend looked at me in some puzzlement; I was not usually so forthcoming. "She's a professional, Joan. You can see that yourself. She's got a nice, spirited style. I like it."

"She's cute. That's what she is."

My friend shrugged. "I heard Janet Reed is interested in her." Janet Reed was the New York City Ballet's ballet mistress at the time.

"You heard what?"

"Janet Reed's so tiny herself."

"But I'm *better* than she is!"

"About the same technically, I'd say," said my friend with a wry smile. "But you're only a student, and that's what you look like. A student. Don't kid yourself."

Suki was taken into the company very quickly, no more than a week or so after she arrived at the school, and the old jealousies I'd suffered were nothing compared with the new ones. San Francisco had been Suki's ground and she'd beaten me on it, but New York was my ground—I got there first—and she'd beaten me on it too. In the months that followed, she became for me the personification of whatever I failed in and a portent for my future; the sight of her in the studios always upset me.

I carried this jealousy around with me always, as a middle-aged junkie carries a habit acquired when young, with loathing and more than a touch of fear; but I could not shake it, and so, although Suki herself was as friendly to me as ever—and doubtless unaware of the extent of the turmoil she caused—I avoided her whenever I could. Sometime during the previous year I'd ceased getting pleasure out of ballet performances, anyway. The stories, if there were stories, seemed tawdry; if there was no story, I could hardly keep my attention on the stage. The male dancers interested me some, but only as athletes; their artistry seemed superfluous to me and their mannerisms often foolish. As for the females, if they were not as technically proficient as I was, they irritated me; if they were more so, they depressed me. When Suki danced her first small solo, I stopped going to the ballet altogether.

It was not long after that that she got polio. Like most people I knew, she had been inoculated against the disease; if she had not been, she might well have died. As it was, she appeared in class one day, pale and weak after a long illness; she moved somewhat tentatively, and it was not until she began the center work that I realized her right shoulder was paralyzed. She lifted her arms to fifth position above her head, but the right one wouldn't go; it stopped halfway, settling down just above her forehead. She had to pull it up with the left, as though it were a dead thing, and it stayed there then only momentarily, indecisively, before drifting down again. Watching her, I was struck with a wave of self-hatred, and of genuine admiration too, despite myself, and after class I sought her out to suggest she get in touch with Carola Trier, who had so much experience in repairing paralysis. Suki said she had been going to Carola for a week already, and I had nothing else to offer her.

It seemed to me, in fact, that I had little to offer anyone in the ballet world anymore. The details of diet and chiropody—basic concerns of the trade I had chosen—began to lose their interest for me. I no longer really cared whether or not Frieda had to use suppositories every five days in her fight with the dancer's old enemy constipation; I listened politely to Elaine's claims that Madame Doubrovska talked about her to Mr. B., but I no longer really heard; even the harshly accurate evaluations meted out to newcomers, in which I had once delighted, began to grate. The sound of giggling and flat Bronx accents, discussions about knitting patterns and the fit of toe shoes, the frequent

tears, the chewing of carrots and the sipping of yogurt—my head seemed to me full of fungal growths,
and I listened as little as I could to these things, with-
drawing instead to a corner of the dressing room to
savor on my own the atmosphere of anxiety that
seemed to be the school's lifeblood.

Such was my mood when I saw Miranda again. It
was the second summer I'd spent in New York, and it
was so hot that out-of-state students occasionally
fainted in class. The studios teemed with out-of-state
students. They came in droves for the summer session
just as they had come to the San Francisco Ballet
School. And just as in San Francisco, an efficient staff
accepted their money and herded them into class-
rooms to extract their hopes. Most of these girls
lacked both talent and training, and few of them were
aware of what they lacked until they had taken class a
week or so. They had been fed on small-town promises
and the praise of inadequately trained teachers; the
sound of muffled sobbing was almost constant in the
dressing room throughout the weeks of summer session, and most of the year-round students dressed as
quickly as they could after class in order to escape into
the heavy, humid air of the city streets outside.

Miranda looked to me still much as she had looked
when I first met her, some seven years before, in
Wanda Wenninger's little studio in Albany, when she
was only eleven and I was only twelve. Her face was
still rosy-cheeked and her hair still covered her ears in
fluffy blond curls; she looked, standing among the girls
I had become used to, like a soft, woolly toy. We
talked a little; she didn't really understand what sort of
class she'd been put in, and she was kind and self-
deprecatory, girding herself, plainly, for the pain she
was sure her presence was going to cause me. She had
come, after all and at long last, for her vindication,
hers and Miss Wanda's.

Like all the school's regular students, I had a

smooth, hard, athlete's body, delineated, spare, clean; I could roll the muscles on my abdomen as though I were a body-builder—it was a technique a number of us had acquired for fun—and there was not an ounce of spare fat on me anywhere. Miranda was a little pudgy, shapeless in the way a child is shapeless, bland and rounded, a Victorian miss on a faded postcard from the seaside. She seemed unaware of the disparity between us, and she tried as best she could to put me at my ease; Miss Wanda's vague vengefulness was not part of her nature, and even at this moment of what she plainly viewed as triumph, she was unhappy at the hurt she thought she was about to inflict.

Like so many other summer students, she had such high hopes that it took several classes for her to grasp the reality of her situation. She was, in this world of professionally trained students, a rank beginner, and even without my glasses I could sense the bewilderment in her when she came one day to watch my class. She didn't cry afterward. She asked me very deferentially if she might talk to me, and I, awash with guilt, told her to meet me in the coffee shop across the street. We drank coffee together in silence, neither one of us able to open the conversation. When I could bear it no longer, I reached out across the table and touched her hand. "I'm sorry, Miranda," I said.

She shook her head impatiently. "All those years," she said. "When I think of the nonsense I believed . . ."

"It doesn't matter, Miranda."

"Yes, it does. It matters terribly. It was my whole life. That's what I thought. My whole life." She sighed. "I don't think she had any idea what she was doing." I kept my eyes on my cup. There was a pause. "You think she knew."

"Yes," I said. "Yes, and no too."

"She was always so kind. I never paid for my lessons, you know. She always gave them free and she always gave me extra ones, and she always told me how Muriel Stuart—" She broke off and shook her head again. "I asked Miss Stuart about her. I—"

"I know. She never heard of her."

"Oh, Joan, what am I going to do?"

"I wouldn't waste money here if I were you. Even if you had the technique, it wouldn't be the place for you." She looked at me a little wildly and then covered her face with her hands. "Look, Miranda," I said, "this is a tough place. It's not nice at all. I'm not nice, either, not like I used to be. At least you're still a decent human being. We're animals here, all of us— big, strong, stupid, domestic animals—like dogs." She opened her mouth to protest, and I hurried on. "We scrabble and scratch at each other. Bite, snap, growl. Day after day. And you know what we're doing it for? Do you know what it's all about?" I laughed, feeling a little wild myself. "He wants us mindless—don't shake your head, that's what he says himself—and that's what everybody here tries to be. After all, if you were a violinist, would you want a violin with a mind of its own?"

"Well, a lot of violinists—" she began tentatively.

"Don't give me that, Miranda. That's crap."

"Why do you say that? You're such a lovely dancer. You don't do yourself justice, Joan. I watched—"

"Are you still interested in poetry?" I asked, rather more abruptly than I had intended. My hands were trembling, and I hid them in my lap.

She smiled and then nodded slowly. "Browning," she said. "Especially Browning."

"I never liked Browning much."

"Why not? You should. It's probably just that you only read him at school. They choose all the dull poems. Why don't you try him? I'm sure you'd like him now."

"I seem to have gone soft in the head. I hardly read at all anymore. I'm always tired."

"Oh, but you can read Browning, I'm sure. Perhaps he'll cheer you up. You're really very lucky, you know." We talked a little longer. I said again that she should go home; Berkeley wasn't an expensive university for a state resident, and I was sure, I told her, that she would enjoy it there, among people who liked poems and weren't too tired to think. Some months afterward a package arrived from her, a small, charmingly bound volume of Browning, delicate and a little faded, like a postcard from a Victorian seaside resort.

7

The intermediate jumps are elegant things, slower, higher off the floor, more dramatic than the small jumps, calling for a fully registered position in the air and usually for what is known as a "sustained landing"—a difficult feat in which, on alighting, the dancer holds position, often on one foot, for as long as a bar or two before the next step.

"OH, BALANCHINE! He was glorious!" My friend Germaine Ogier had known him, along with Danilova and Doubrovska and the others, during her years at the Ballet Russe. "He came to the studio with a man with white hair, and I remember thinking, My goodness, you're absolutely gorgeous! He just stood there and watched class for about an hour; he couldn't have been very old then and his carriage was marvelous. I was out of my mind in love with him. Each time he appeared, I'd think, Oh, there's that lovely man again! and I kept on prancing in front of him, hoping his eye would light on me. He was so fascinating!

"He did two ballets when I was in the company, *La Concurrence* and *Cotillon,* and he was absolutely charming and never disagreeable. He used to compliment us occasionally, and we were used to people being very—well, not nice. But he was nice to everyone, nice and polite and gentle. And he was, as you say,

Joan, very, very technical. He did exercises I'd never seen before—*grand battement* with your foot up—and his tempo was a bit different. I'd never done exercises single time and then double time before; that could well have been an innovation of his. But he hadn't started changing technique yet."

Balanchine is quite a small man; I hadn't expected that. But aside from his stature and his pronounced tic, he looked very much the embodiment of what was for me, as for many young dancers, a godhead. I had never seen him before he entered a class I was about to take one day early in my time at his school; I recognized him immediately even without my glasses, partly from the unaccustomed hush that fell over my fellows and partly because he walked, or so it seemed, in an atmosphere all his own. There was a quiet about his person, as though the air were stiller there where it touched him; he was, from that first glimpse of him to my last, the most naturally elegant human being I ever laid eyes on.

Perhaps because of his tic, or because of his efforts to control it, he breathed through his mouth, and he spoke often through an intake of air, which whistled against his teeth, blurring his words a little as though he had a lisp. His voice was always low, intimate without being familiar—a chamber music voice instead of an orchestral one—unexpectedly audible, soothing, gentle, but animated too, excited even when he got caught up in explaining something; his English was lightly accented and wholly fluent, without any hint of the comic-opera Russian that Danilova and Doubrovska spoke. And he was, as Germaine said, flawlessly polite. Nor was there any inflection of noblesse oblige or any smell of the deportment class about him; he was polite with a natural grace that matched his natural elegance or perhaps grew out of it.

It was an extraordinary tribute to his manner that in a place like the School of American Ballet, where the slightest physical flaws are joyously and routinely ridiculed, nobody spoke about his tic, although it was impossible not to notice it. Every few minutes the central inch of his upper lip lifted suddenly, spasmodically, two or three times in quick succession, as though retracted by a malevolent puppeteer; his front teeth and the canines and the wet gum above lay bare for an instant and then disappeared again, appeared and were gone, appeared and were gone, like individual frames from a film. As a child in Saint Petersburg he had been nicknamed Rat; the taunt was descriptive, but to all of us irrelevant.

Beyond the simple fact of being in the presence of George Balanchine himself, though, I didn't much care for the class he taught that day, or for most of the other classes I took from him. He was not a teacher to study under all the time, in any case; he was too much a theorist to deal with the practical necessities of building technique and too much a perfectionist to be of much help in contributing to the dancer's almost infinite need for more strength. I hated to admit it, but I was bored. An entire hour was given over to *pliés;* he spoke of the pros and cons of this and that placement, of just precisely at what musical interstice the heels should leave the floor, of just precisely how much stretch could be got out of an Achilles tendon, or just precisely how much a turn-out could be pushed. After the class everybody felt somewhat let down; it was literally impossible to do what he wanted as he wanted it. And if we could not do what he wanted, what did that leave us with?

The only class of his I remember enjoying was not taught for the benefit of his students but designed instead to serve as a photographic session with Henri Cartier-Bresson, and the pictures hung afterward in the City Center theater. It was plain that Balanchine was not entirely at ease during that class, but only to those of us whom he had taught before. He did not explain endlessly; he did not pick at the minutiae of

any one step or exercise as he always had; he cor-
rected us more or less after the manner of our usual
teachers, and the class moved fairly quickly from
barre to center work; he wasn't really concentrating,
but no more obvious trace of nervousness showed.
Meantime, in contrast to his subject's cool, fine-
grained elegance, Cartier-Bresson tiptoed around the
room, under raised legs and between sweating bodies,
bouncing up and down a little, like an actor in the
bedroom of a French farce. He got down on his hands
and knees and aimed his camera self-consciously this
way and that; he crawled about on all fours underfoot;
he lay on his belly and rolled over on his back, while
his stalwart assistant carried and placed the heavier
equipment according to his fluttering and petulant directions. Each movement he made looked pretentious
to me, practiced, so self-concerned that I was sure his
pictures would have a weak and foolish elaborateness
to them that could not possibly do justice to his subject.

In that assessment I could not have been more
wrong; no other pictures I have seen of Balanchine
convey so well the quality I remember. Others tend to
romanticize him when he needs no romanticizing or to
make him look ordinary when he is by no means ordinary; in these pictures alone it is possible to glimpse
the elegance, the intensity, the natural aristocracy of
bearing that is so peculiarly his own. And the best of
them shows him with his eyes on me.

I had no idea that he had paid me any attention at all;
the picture came as a complete surprise. Dexter took
me to a performance of something at the City Center,
and he was the one who noticed the picture hanging
there. I confirmed delightedly that the object of Balanchine's attention was indeed me, and Dexter took it on
himself to order a copy for each of us from a friend of
his at Magnum, Cartier-Bresson's picture agency.

"But don't you think," he said, holding up his hand

to cover an inch or so at the right-hand side of the picture, "that all these extraneous hands spoil the balance?"

The Magnum man explained that Cartier-Bresson kept his negatives in France, and the developing would be done in Paris to order.

"In that case," Dexter said, "tell them to crop the right-hand side by an inch, will you?"

There was a heavy pause. "Cartier-Bresson does not crop," the Magnum man said coldly.

The pictures arrived and we trimmed them to please ourselves. A few years later, a biography of Balanchine came out and that very photograph appeared on the cover. The right-hand side had been cropped almost precisely according to Dexter's suggestion.

While Balanchine did not often teach, his presence pervaded the school. There was no aspect of our lives that we did not revise in the light of what we took to be his views. As I've said, we wore heavy makeup because Doubrovska said he liked pretty girls, and we made ourselves foolish because several periodicals had quoted him as saying dancers were stupid. Beyond these, we questioned nothing because he told us not to analyze when he taught us; we knew hardly anything about each other's lives because he was interested in us as dancers, not as people, and where his interest in us left off, ours in each other did too. We were, or felt ourselves to be, precisely what one of his principals once said of herself and his other dancers: "chosen creatures," and we were proud of it. Such slavishness was as demeaning outside the classroom as it was, perhaps, inevitable; inside the classroom, however, it was both a necessity and a privilege. During the period I spent as a pupil in New York, Balanchine made a number of changes in basic technique which combined to alter the American style considerably, and we were in on the very beginning.

The changes were not introduced to us by Balanchine himself; he left that to Doubrovska. Every once in a while after floating across the studio on tiptoe, her tulle scarf wafting out behind her and her doll-like face full of apology and self-doubt, she would clear her throat daintily and say, "Mr. Balanchine has decided . . ."

The first thing that Mr. Balanchine decided, as I remember it, was to alter the all-important fifth position. Fifth position is traditionally formed by crossing the fully turned-out feet so that only the last joint of the big toe on the back foot peeps out; it is a tricky position to hold. Under pressure it tends to loosen and become a third and then a first; and even, in poorly trained or not fully trained dancers, a demi-second. The harsh chant "Fifth! Fifth! Fifth!" echoes throughout every ballet studio on every continent. What Balanchine decided to try was fully crossing the feet to begin with so that not even the big-toe joint showed; the theory was that if a dancer began with such a very tight fifth, her feet would move to the traditional fifth under pressure and then perhaps to a third, but not as far as a first. It took some months for the school to absorb the change, which involves a basic shift in weight and balance despite its trivial sound; but Mr. Balanchine had decided, and in the end, his decision brought about almost precisely the result he had foreseen it would.

Balanchine also decided we should wear old toe shoes to class every day; pointe classes concentrate almost entirely on the range of steps done only on toe shoes, and many pupils find it difficult, after wearing slippers to regular class, to jump and balance in glue-stiffened shoes on the stage. We were not allowed to remove the heavy shanks; balancing was almost impossible at first, and we wavered as though perched on a single, motionless ice skate. But Mr. Balanchine had decided, and little by little we grew stronger and surer.

Most important were his alterations to the jumps. He made two basic decisions about them, and it was Carol Sumner, as I mentioned earlier, who inspired the first. Carol looked light, airborne, easy, when she jumped. The rest of us looked heavy and a little clumsy beside her, as did every member of the company. And she managed this quality in spite of a serious technical flaw: she could not get her heels down to the ground immediately on landing from a jump. The flaw is almost universal in elementary students but largely absent in advanced ones; it was a great pity, we all agreed, even though Carol's version was plainly peculiar to herself. Everybody else whose heels come off the floor looks messy to a trained eye; Carol's work was unusually neat, and in all steps other than jumps—turns and the like—her heels were solidly on the ground when they were supposed to be. It was a puzzle we discussed from time to time, always to the conclusion of a shrug and a sigh. Balanchine was plainly interested too. He watched her carefully, and after a few months Doubrovska told us that Mr. Balanchine had decided we were all to jump with our heels off the floor.

It is difficult to get across just how radical a departure this decision was, both from tradition and from all the accepted theories concerning allegro work. Jumping from a semitiptoe position is as repellent to a dancer's eye as misplaced modifiers are to a grammarian's, and one of the most difficult things a ballet student learns is to keep her heels down when she takes off for and lands from a jump. The great Preobrajenska was, as my friend Germaine, who studied under her, told me, a "maniac" on the subject of keeping the heels down. The Christensens were the same, and so was the staff at the School of American Ballet. The seemingly endless shout of "Heels! Heels! Heels!" was even more frequent, if possible, than "Fifth! Fifth! Fifth!" It simply never occurred to anyone of us that Carol looked light *because* of her technical flaw; we assumed that had she been able to get her heels down, she would have looked all the better for it, and we were, I must admit, more than a little shocked by

Balanchine's decision. But he had decided and we did what we could to obey.

At first the results were comical. We stumbled drunkenly; we turned our ankles; we developed stone bruises; there were giggles and tears, heated discussions and angry frustrations. But slowly, slowly, over a period of about six weeks, we developed an airy ease just like Carol's, all of us. We came to have that rare quality heretofore seen only in dancers born with it and now common to all Americans. We were enchanted. Balanchine was pleased with us; Doubrovska told us so.*

The second element in the now typical American dancer's jump came about in a somewhat more piecemeal fashion. Doubrovska told us one day that Balanchine had decided that we were to make the *pas de chat* a big jump. The *pas de chat* used to look much like its name, a cat step, if the cat is seen from the side springing over a minor obstacle in its path. The dancer takes the movement face on; she jumps with the right knee bent—if she's moving to the right—then straightens the right in the air while bending the left. It was a quick step, a pretty thing that displayed speed and precision. But Balanchine had decided that it was to be taken as a big jump, a leap of sorts; furthermore, he had decided that instead of moving the legs as the cat does, in tandem, we were to try to hit something akin to a cross-legged tailor position in the air. And not only were we to hit this position, we were supposed to look as though we were sustaining it in midair. This, as Doubrovska explained to us as best she could, was an

---

*It is worth noting that the trick works only on those who have been trained fully to get their heels down *first;* the heels do, as Carol's did, hit the ground, but they do so fractionally late. The entirety of the body's weight is shifted forward almost to the point of off-balance, so that the jump is, in effect, sustained momentarily on *demi-pointe* before the ensuing *plié*—in which the heels make contact with the floor as usual—is completed.

optical illusion we were to achieve by fractionally tightening the position—bringing the legs up toward the crotch just ever so little—at the height of the jump. As with all of Mr. Balanchine's decisions, this one had precisely the effect he'd anticipated; we looked as though we were jumping higher than we had before and we looked almost as though we hovered in the air for a fraction of a second before alighting. Gradually he applied the same, or similar, techniques to all the big jumps.

I recently told a gifted young English girl I know that I would teach her, when she was advanced enough, how to jump as I had been taught. Her eyes widened. "You mean like an American?" she said. "But they're so light. They jump so high. Will you really? Any English dancer who can do things like that guards her secret with her life."

8

The big jumps, the leaping and turning in the air that are ballet's most exciting steps, come at the end of class; they represent not only the culmination of all the effort that has preceded them, but its meaning and reward as well: it is here that real power makes itself felt.

BALLET SCHOOLS, like society balls, run on atmosphere; there was tension in the air the morning I was apprenticed, and everybody felt it. The secretaries spoke too brightly; the girls in the Special Class tittered nervously, and Doubrovska, when she floated across the floor to teach class, dropped her filmy scarf in the middle of the room, where it lay for one startling moment, pale mauve and lifeless on the floor. It was either Rosemary or me—we exchanged glances from our positions at the barre—or possibly both of us. No one had any idea which; none of us knew precisely how the rite of passage was effected, either, what signs were made, what words spoken. Apprentices kept this Secret to themselves, this vertex on the celebrant's curve; other people learned about it only afterward, and only by signs.

Halfway through the barre, Balanchine entered the

studio, as elegant as ever in shirtsleeves rolled to his elbows; he didn't speak to Doubrovska and she didn't speak to him. As though alone in the room, he sat in the middle of the bench that ran all along the wall of mirrors, and she got up to demonstrate the next exercise without so much as a nod in his direction. She roamed the room restlessly then, touching one student's shoulder into place here and another student's foot into position there; she peered into my face to see if I had put on makeup according to her directions some months back, and smiled her approval that I had. Balanchine bowed his head and hid his face in his hands, supporting his elbows on his knees. The adagio work was, I thought unhappily, designed to show off Rosemary, who had excellent balance. But the jumps were mine. My elevation was almost a man's, and Doubrovska arranged the exercises well, or so it seemed to me, to show me off. Balanchine remained motionless, head bowed, throughout.

After class I waited in a more or less public passageway; I thought I would be easier to find there than in the dressing room, and Janet Reed, the ballet mistress, sat down beside me.

"Just finished class?" she said. She'd never spoken to me before, nor, for that matter, ever acknowledged my existence. I knew who she was, no more, but her tone was friendly and warm. I nodded. She smiled. Neither of us said anything for a moment. Then she turned to me as though suddenly struck with an ingenious idea. "Hey, Joan," she said, "I wonder if you'd be willing to help us out." I nodded again. "We're short a dancer," she went on, "and there isn't much time left. Would you give it a try?" I nodded once more. The ballet was *Stars and Stripes,* which I'd never seen; the first performance was in four days. A rehearsal had been set up for me in an hour. They were very grateful. And as soon as I entered the dressing room I knew Rosemary had been apprenticed too, and in the same ballet; she was to dance in the First Regiment, the corps of short girls, and I in the Second, with the taller girls.

The rehearsal consisted of myself, a coach and a pianist in the same small room that had served for my audition nearly two years before; it lasted an hour, and by the end of it I had some idea of what I was supposed to do. Like most Balanchine ballets, *Stars and Stripes* is hard on the corps; the steps are difficult technically, the part is long, and the involvements with other dancers complicated. But there were no other dancers now; there was only me. "You do this," my coach said, "while here on your right, So-and-so does that. Then you move downstage this way and pass between So-and-so on your right and So-and-so on your left." I knew a few of the names. "And then you do *jetés élancés* in a circle. What? You've never done them before? Well, look," and she began to teach me, but a *jeté élancé* is a big jump that requires space, and the room was too small. "Oh, never mind. Just follow So-and-so. She's right in front of you. And then . . ."

After the rehearsal I went to Sam Goody's West Side outlet, as my coach had suggested, to buy a record of the music. "You won't hear the orchestra live until the performance," she said, "and it doesn't sound the same as a piano. The tempo on the record will be different, but at least it'll give you some idea what the music's like." Sam Goody's had had a copy of *Stars and Stripes* an hour before I got there, but it had been sold—to Rosemary, as it turned out. The salesman was kindly; he promised to get me one in two days. I telephoned Rosemary; she couldn't afford, she said, to lend me the record. Not even for an hour. She was sorry.

Several other stores I tried had nothing in stock, either, and so, feeling much put upon, I took the train to my mother's apartment in Mount Vernon. She had asked me to dinner and she greeted me warmly, expressing pleasure and excitement at the news of my apprenticeship.

"And the first performance is in a week?"

"I wish it were," I said. "Thursday. Three days now."

"Thursday? Good God, how can you possibly be ready? Why can't you borrow Rosemary's record? Oh, she can't, can't she? So you're going to have to learn all those transitions or whatever on the very day—the same day—you perform the thing?" She seemed appalled. "What I don't understand," she went on, "is why you have anything to do with such a profession."

I laughed and gestured at the pages of my father's manuscript, which lay on the table where she had been working. "You don't seem to have chosen your profession very well, either. Don't you ever rest?"

The weary hunch of her shoulders was, I noticed, more pronounced than when I'd seen her last; she pressed her hand over her eyes from time to time too, as though they stung, and she sighed almost continually. My father's old colleagues were dragging their feet over publication, she said. "They don't care. They don't really want to do it. The only one who cares is me, and I'll be damned if I'll let them kill this book."

From his chair my father reached over and patted her arm. "Oh, poor," he said. "Oh, poor."

"But it's not really you, Joanie," she said abruptly, taking hold of my father's hand but directing her glance at me. "All this tension and uncertainty. You were never good under tension. Performing isn't really your—"

"Let's not talk about that part of it. Not now, anyway. Could I take a bath? Do you mind? I feel all sweaty."

"I see," she said. Her voice went cold, and I looked at her, puzzled. "You don't even want to talk to me about it. I suppose you can talk to Dexter, though. Is that it?"

"Oh, Mother, let's not fight."

"I'm not fighting. I merely asked a question."

"Look, I'm sorry. I just don't—"

She got up, went into the bathroom and ran water into the tub. "I thought you wanted to take a bath," she said a few minutes later. "Don't you get undressed to bathe these days?"

She leaned against the doorjamb. I undressed and washed in silence. "Why don't you come back and live with us, Joanie?" she said, as abrupt in her plea as she had been in her anger. "We could get an apartment in the city and you could . . . I'm sorry I get mad at you. I can't help it sometimes. It hurts me to think of you— so young—with old people all the time. Don't you want to see people your own age sometimes?"

"I do see them. Every day."

"I don't mean dancers. I mean thinking people, people who might be your friends. Don't you want friends your own age? Dexter ought to be living with an old woman like me, and you know it. You'll get bored with each other after a while, anyway, and then it'll be too late. You'll be old too."

"I don't care," I said, suddenly angry myself. "I'll live with him as long as he'll have me. I feel alive when I'm with him. When I'm not, I feel dead. Is that what you want for me?"

She drew her tongue along her upper lip and looked me over slowly from head to foot and back again. "You know, Joanie," she said, drawing her body up and running her hands down the front of the well-cut woolen jacket she had on, "you've got the breasts of a woman of forty. They sag as though you'd had half a dozen kids. Have you ever noticed that?"·

I pulled myself out of the bath, dressed, and went back to New York. We did not even say goodbye.

The entire company rehearsed *Stars and Stripes* in the morning, but Rosemary and I alone danced; the others of our respective regiments merely walked through their parts. Balanchine, who directed, taught me quickly and easily how to do the step my coach of the day before had been unable to teach, and the rehearsal was over. I pleaded with Rosemary to let me listen to her record, but she remained adamant; she did not really know her part, either.

By noon on Wednesday my position seemed hopeless. I had hardly slept since my visit to Mount Vernon; I could not rid myself of the uneasy feeling that some sort of disaster would come of my mother's behavior. That evening, though, Sam Goody's produced a copy of the record. I took it with me to Dexter's apartment, listened to it several times and was reassured. I had almost the whole of Thursday ahead of me; with the notes I'd made and with several hours of practice with the music, I would be ready.

I spent the night with Dexter, who left at seven Thursday morning; there was an early meeting at Consumers Union that he and my mother had to attend. As soon as he was gone I got out the record, and at eight o'clock, when I had more or less established just what I needed to work on, the doorbell rang. I went to answer it, sweating and irritable. My mother stood there in the hallway. Her arms hung down from the hunch in her shoulders like cast-off sleeves, and her eyes were hooded. She'd driven all the way into the city to see me, she said; she'd skipped the meeting to do it. There was, she went on, some unfinished business between us, and wasn't I going to ask her in? I backed away. She closed the door behind her. "Well," she said, "here we are. Aren't you going to ask your mother to sit down in your lover's living room?"

My hesitation seemed to irritate her. "What's the matter with you, anyway? Scared? Well, it's no wonder, is it?" Again she paused and again I could think of no reply. This time my silence seemed simply to enrage her, and the words came out like drumbeats.

"Well, you damn well ought to be scared. You're no performer. How can you possibly think you can get out on a stage and do anything? You're nothing but a sniveling little tart, shacked up with a man who'll throw you out when he's finished with you. Don't deny it. I know him, after all. You can't think he really cares anything about you, do you? You with those saggy breasts of yours. He likes women who are interested in something. You're not interested in anything. When's the last time you read a book? What have you got to say to a man like that? Don't look to me for help when he's finished with you. And don't think you're going to be a dancer, either. You're not good enough and you know it. I know it. You don't even know that silly little part. You'll never know it. You haven't the wit to learn it. Nothing goes into your head anymore. Even if you knew it, you couldn't do it. You look like death on a stage. Who wants to watch death? One performance, and that'll be the end of you. You'll never dance. Not ever."

The skin of my cheeks tingled. The voice seemed to reach me from a great distance and, finally, through a claustrophobic darkness into which it squeezed alongside my chest so that I felt it throbbing against my rib cage. And then, miraculously, it stopped. I lay on one of Carola Trier's spring-loaded exercise beds; there were spasms like hiccups where the voice had been, and my arms seemed to have grown so long that my hands were out of sight. Everything felt heavy, drugged, slow.

"Come on, Joan," Carola was saying. "It's all over now. You're all right. You're going to be fine." My sister Judy, who had come to New York the year before to go to the Art Students League, sat beside me on the thin plastic-covered mat. I have no idea—none whatever—how she'd managed to get me to Carola's or how she had come to find me in the first place.

Sometime later I drank orange juice and glanced at the window. It was nearly evening. The day was gone, and I did not know my part. My voice was gone too; when I tried to speak, only grunts and croaks came out, and I could not tell them what was wrong.

In the corps dressing room at the theater, I was assigned a place at a long table, a far grander affair than I'd ever encountered before, with naked bulbs around the mirrors like dressing tables in the movies; my hat stood beside me. I had been told nothing about the hat. It was eighteen inches high, a black top hat, with a strap to secure it under the chin. I had no idea how I was going to keep it on, and I turned it from side to side, watching, as I did so, the wry smile of the dancer next to me. I opened my mouth to speak, but only a guttural sound emerged. She giggled while I did what I could with bobby pins along the strap. She giggled again when I put on my socks. I hadn't expected them, either; they were over the pink tights to suggest boots, and they made my toe shoes slip. I soaked my heels in water.

The costumes were tutus, fancied up to look like a cheerleader's uniform. In San Francisco we had dressed ourselves, helping each other with hard-to-reach zippers. In the costume room at City Center there were a dozen women in flowered smocks, who were called dressers; union regulations, they told me severely, said no performer could touch his costume; they chose one for me from rows of spares. Thus dressed, hatted and socked, I stood in the passageway, trying to remember my part, but I could remember nothing, not even what I had remembered in my two rehearsals. I had to pee very badly.

The dressers sat drinking coffee. I made a noise in my throat, and one of them looked up. "Well?" she said. I shifted from foot to foot. "Oh, God, it's one of the new ones. Well, do it in your costume, baby. I done my duty by you."

In my desperation I began to unzip my costume myself, and all dozen of them leaped for me in a body. "You can't do that," they said. "O.K., O.K., we'll take it off."

As in my San Francisco days, I hardly peed at all; the dressers grumbled and redressed me. I was halfway down the hall when I had to pee again. And again and again. The dressers began laying bets on how many times more were possible, but they became friendly too. "You mustn't take it so hard, dearie." "Most of um are like that at first." "Don't shake like that, honey, you'll never be able to stand up on your toes if you do."

In the dark backstage I felt a gentle touch on my shoulder and turned to find Suki beside me, standing on pointe so that her face was level with mine. Carola had built new muscles in her back, and her once paralyzed arm was wholly functional again. *"Merde,"* she whispered into my ear, licking two fingers and wiping their damp tips on my arm in the traditional good luck gesture. "You'll be all right, Joanie. Just be sure to smile as hard as you can."

The Second Regiment formed backstage and went on; I went too, grinning horribly. Within the first eight bars I was lost; a voice called to me to go here and go there. I did not know who it was. My body felt leaden and stupid, and then during the jumps that Balanchine himself had taught me my high top hat edged down over my eyes. I flipped a hand at it. It settled toward the back of my neck, wobbling unsurely, then swung down over my eyes again. When my left shoe slipped off my heel, though, there were only a few bars to go and I was near the back.

I waited in the wings for the finale, frozen in the knowledge of my failure; Allegra Kent, the principal that evening, exited at stage front and came up behind me. I heard her there but I could not move. She was out of breath, panting, gasping a little; she tried to pass me first on the right, then on the left, and again on the right, skittering behind my immobile back like a trapped mouse and making soft whimpering sounds. At last she reached out and moved me bodily with ice-cold fingers that trembled against my skin.

Suki affixed my hat with strong hairpins and put rosin in between my socks and tights so my shoes wouldn't slip. The finale began. It was an easier section, and I remembered it, but there was a lift at the end of it, which, because the company rehearsal had not included the finale, I had not been able to practice. At the climactic moment somebody hoisted me upward, but his timing and mine were not in concert; he swore and dropped me as the curtain closed. There were six performances to go.

In class the next morning, Doubrovska kissed Rosemary and said, "You do well, Rosemary. Very strong. In control. You might, maybe, smile a little more happy, but is nice. Good girl." She turned toward me, and a hush fell over the others, all of whom had attended the performance. "Now, John," she said, shaking her head sadly, "why you not ask girl next to you how to put on hat, John? Years you study how to dance. Then time comes to dance and you don't ask how to put on hat. And shoes. Shoes too. Why?" She took hold of my arm and peered into my face. "And you don't know part, John. You must learn part before tomorrow. That is not right, not to know part. Yes?" She smiled. "But you smile. Is not your prettiest smile, but you smile." And then dropping her voice so I alone could hear, she whispered, "If boy drops you, John, you kick. He won't do again. I speak to him myself; I tell him *I* tell you to kick."

When the New York season was over, Rosemary went into the company and the company went on tour, leaving me behind as it had left the redheaded girl behind when I first entered the school. I took her position at the top of the ranking, assured of my position in the company and yet not sure of it. A week before the company was due to return, I walked out of the school and didn't come back.

I entered Columbia University as an undergraduate that fall, and for my first two months as a college student I took ballet classes at Carnegie Hall, where I had gone occasionally during my last year at Balanchine's school. There was a teacher there whom I liked particularly, a slender, dapper Englishman with too much red in his hair dye; he always wore white: white shoes, white pants, white shirt. He'd never spoken to me much, a few corrections here and there, but his bearing and his teaching had a calm formality that appealed to me after the tension and flamboyance of the Russians.

The morning of the last class I took in New York, I sat in the hallway outside the studio with my books spread out on the floor in front of me; I hadn't seen him approach, and I looked up only when his shadow fell across the page I was reading.

"Studying?" he said. I nodded. "I've been meaning to ask you for a couple of weeks now," he said, and then bit his lip. "I mean, have you had a bit of luck lately?" I looked puzzled, and he went on. "It's just that—well, you always had a good technique, but you used to be, you know, just a little flat. It's none of my business, really, but all of a sudden you *look* like a dancer. Has something changed?"

"I guess so," I said, laughing. "I've given up dancing."

"Altogether? No more Balanchine?" I nodded. He shook his head and sighed. "And I thought you'd got a good part at last. It sometimes happens, you know— that flowering—sometimes when there's a good part. Ah, well, never mind. Given up entirely?" I nodded once more. "For the books? I see," he said, smiling. "I see."

PART III

1

Pointe work is a dancer's finishing touch, the bloom on her art; the risk of injury from the technique is, however, constant, and training must be very slow at first and very skillful throughout if she is not to carry the marks of such an unnatural stance for the rest of her life.

THE NEW YORK CITY REGISTRY OFFICE has a special room in which marriages are performed; there are pews for waiting couples like the pews in waiting rooms of public clinics. In front of them, where the administrative nurse's desk ought to be, stands a dollhouse chapel, just large enough for Herman Katz—registrar for New York at the time—a happy couple and one witness. Dexter and I had two witnesses and the fit was very tight. A plastic stained-glass window threw a saintly light as Mr. Katz read out his official pronouncement in a funereal voice. The pronouncement took no more than five minutes; we signed our names to a certificate, Mr. Katz signed his, and that was that. We had breakfast at the Plaza afterward. It was a lovely fall day; the martinis were cold and dry; the eggs Benedict were perfectly cooked; our witnesses, a pianist and a man in movies, made fine companions. It was a delightful wedding.

I continued on at Columbia University after it, taking courses in philosophy and arguing the meaning of self over beer and French fries at the West End Bar with animated friends, young men and women who were never tired and who didn't care about calories or bunions or knitting patterns. I veered in the direction of Continental existentialism, wading eagerly if laboriously through glutinous passages on life and death in Heidegger and Husserl and Sartre; my friends were drawn mostly to the involuted word puzzles and serpentine logic of the Oxford dons: the beer was cold and the talk excited, and I liked their unmannered gestures, their slightly stooped carriages and the groping intensity in their voices.

At home, I went over the same ground with Dexter, whose fascination with the direction of physics and the evils of commerce gave a tangible reality to what I'd heard in the classroom and the bar; I put scrambled eggs behind me and learned to make a many-layered French omelet for us to eat while we talked, sitting, as we usually did, at a pretty round table that looked out over the park to the Hudson River through the huge oak-mullioned windows of our apartment on Riverside Drive. We often sat there until well into the night—sometimes until the bright red of the SPRY sign on the Palisades grew dim and it was morning again.

Occasionally, as the night wore on, or the morning drew in, I became tearful, especially if we'd had a second bottle of wine or drunk an extra brandy or two; my past crowded me then as my father's past had crowded him on Sundays in Berkeley.

"She's your friend," I would say to Dexter. "You tell me. Why didn't she just shoot me instead?"

"Look," he would say, "it's all over with. It's finished. Besides, you were ready to quit anyway."

"I wanted to make my own decision," I'd say, shouting by this time. "What's so strange about that?"

"Nothing. Not a thing. But why can't you bring yourself up to the present? Why get bogged down in something wholly out of reach? And in any case," he would sometimes add, "she wasn't always like that and she isn't only like that."

One afternoon when I was alone with my father in Mount Vernon, I had told him I was marrying Dexter; he seemed to understand, although it may have been only that he heard the happiness in my voice and responded to that. He stroked my hand and said, "Good, good." I didn't tell my mother. At my insistence, Dexter didn't tell her, either. She didn't find out until much later, and by that time the fact was well enough established so that her anger cast only a pale and transient shadow over it.

A year or so after we got married, she called me to the hospital for stroke victims outside New York City where my father had been a patient for some months; the doctors were at last prepared, she told me, to unplug the machine that had done his breathing for him during most of the previous weeks. Dexter took me there and sat with me on a bench in the hallway outside my father's room. My father used to sleep badly, especially in those days just before his stroke, when he and my mother were on such bad terms together; more than once, though, she had awakened to find him clutching at her shoulder. "Mildred," he'd say through his teeth, "when I'm dying, don't leave me. Please." His voice trembled and she could hear the tears in it. "Please, I don't want to die alone." The next morning it was as though the incident had never happened, but she watched over him even so in that room beyond; hour after hour, as he alternately rallied and weakened, deep in coma, she stroked his cheek and brushed the hair away from his eyes. Judy was in Iowa with her new husband; she had morning sickness already. But my uncle, my father's brother, stood watch with my mother; his wife, Patsy, was there too. Patsy had been a nurse and she issued bulletins every forty minutes or so throughout the afternoon, urging me from time to time to come in and say goodbye. The hallway was painted pale gray; it smelled of musk and antiseptic; outside, the day was bright and sunny, and the hospital gardens full of flowers. I shook my head at her each time and held tight to Dexter's hand. Toward evening, my father died.

When my sister Judy and I were small, my mother used to quote, "Life is real and life is earnest/And the grave is not the goal," but her eyes came, in the years after our arrival in New York, to have the aged, marooned resignation of a turtle's eyes. Her heart had developed a swooshing sound after one of her many childhood diseases; she'd frightened doctors with it all her life, and after my father's death she began to suffer fainting spells. She flew into unaccountable rages at work; she insulted old friends; she talked too much and much too loudly. One evening in the middle of July, she dressed herself in a violet suit of soft wool and went to dinner with Consumers Union's president, Colston Warne, and the board's secretary, Helen Nelson, at a restaurant in Scarsdale to discuss some testimony she was preparing to deliver to a congressional committee on the subject of consumer credit; she was, so they said, in fine spirits, and she died right there at the table, midsentence, with a fork halfway to her mouth.

By the time I graduated from Columbia University, I was pregnant, and the powerful ballet dancer's muscles in my abdomen made the condition particularly disagreeable. They held the baby so tight that his feet crowded my stomach and my lungs; I gained only eight pounds during the entire nine months. "Even the pregnant women in Dachau gained weight," said my despairing gynecologist, and when I arrived at the hospital, the admissions secretary, casting an eye over my more or less flat front, directed me firmly to the visitors' elevator. The labor was quick and hard; the dancer's muscles came into their own then and ejected the baby—despite his efforts to be born face up—in under five hours.

We named the child after my father, whose middle name was Alexander, and after a much-loved relative of Dexter's; when the baby was seven months old the three of us left New York. Dexter had resigned as Director of Consumers Union, although he continued to do some editorial consulting jobs of a sort he had done for magazines for years. He'd also won Little, Brown's interest in two books he wanted to write, and the contract he got for them looked very promising. With these supports and all our savings, we decided to see what life was like abroad while Alexander was still young enough for us to move around easily with him. We traveled to Antwerp on a Norwegian freighter named, as though with a goodbye touch of malice, the *Black Swan*. We had not really intended to settle in England—we considered ourselves tourists on a more or less open-ended vacation—but nannies and houses were cheap then. We arranged with a friend to move us out of the apartment on Riverside Drive, while we bought and moved into a house built some thirty years before by Lloyd George for one of his pretty young secretaries. It stood near Hindhead on the Farnham Road, at one edge of the Devil's Punchbowl in Surrey, not more than a mile from the entrance to Lloyd George's house and near a pub called the Pride of the Valley; painted on the sign outside the pub was the former prime minister himself in a black cape, with a big staff in his hand.

"You can always tell one of his houses," said the carpenter, pulling irritably at the rusting hinges of the front door of our house. "They all got these same cheap oak doors. You used to see the old duffer with that staff of his marching up the road, going into one of these houses after another. Take him all morning, it did." He grunted. "The Pride of the Valley, my whiskers! The Shame of the Valley's more like it."

Lloyd George's morning walks must have been long ones; our house was off very much on its own, set back from the road and surrounded by woodland. It had not been lived in for some years, and there was a lot of work to be done. Dexter started in on his novel even so, writing sporadically when we weren't painting walls and sanding floors and pulling well-established bracken out of the vegetable garden. While he wrote, I typed his manuscripts, played with Alexander, and set up reading schedules for myself. The schedules were impressive to look at—history and psychology and religion—but I rarely kept to them. Too often I slipped murder mysteries between the pages of my texts or stared out over the green of the English countryside, watching the light shift among the trees.

In our first few months there in Hindhead, Dexter became much taken with a car he'd seen in the neighborhood, a sleek black Riley already fifteen years old and reminiscent of a 1930s Mafia Packard. We bought it for the astonishing sum of £156, and on sunny days we put aside our books and paintbrushes, bundled up Alexander, and rode in it up over the Surrey hills and through the New Forest where the wild ponies are, by Wendy's Wood and Conan Doyle's house, past Stella's Cottage and the ruins of Sir William Temple's manor, where Dean Swift had helped Sir William prepare his memoirs for publication, over the tiny winding rivers and beside the huge oaks and yews in ancient churchyards. We saw very few people. In the evenings we talked, as we always had, but now we talked in front of a blazing log fire in our living room, from which we looked out over the rolling, tree-covered landscape to the distant Hogs Back, where the lights twinkled until well past midnight. Many times we watched those lights go out, talking on into the night in front of the warmth of the fire about carpenters and plumbers, varieties of paint and fuse wire, about what I'd read and what he'd written, reading out loud to each other from these and from other things, until the blackness outside eased into the gray drizzle that begins most English mornings.

Dexter is a big man, well over six feet, with a huge rib cage and a singer's lung capacity, but slender even so, fine-boned and long-legged; his face is mobile and he has arched and tufted eyebrows not unlike Harold Christensen's. His first wife, Christina, painted him once as a devil in heavy strokes of red and black, and the picture is by no means out of character; the quality when he smiles, though, is puckish rather than evil and when he is angry the devil is gone altogether; he becomes cold and aloof then, like an English lord in a working-class pub, and the ice in his voice is betrayed only by a slight tremor in his hands. His eyes, although he insists they are hazel in color, give the impression of blackness from across a room; the light plays in them in a way I've never noticed in anyone else, a sharp, bright reflection in each eye that gives him a look of keen curiosity such as small wild animals sometimes have in the pages of the *National Geographic*. And yet there's nothing beady in his expression, largely, I suppose, because, like Harold Christensen again, the cast of his face is amused, often mischievous, always changing. The uneven cadences of his speech and its unexpected elisions show the changeableness in him too, the concurrent levels of thought, the shifting colors and intensities, and to this day he sits and he stands as though he weren't entirely comfortable and could never be made so.

One evening around that warm Hindhead fire, I told him how my grandmother, my father's mother, could not bear to teach her children "Now I lay me down to sleep"; the line "And if I die before I wake" might frighten them, she thought, in the dark when they were all alone. She had devised new words that retained the verse's bleak message for an adult listener but masked them from the praying child—something about forests and trees and a faraway place to play. But I could not remember the words and felt very sad. Dexter's chin puckers sometimes, ever so slightly, when he is moved; he frowned to cover it this time as he often does and poured out another glass of wine.

"Let me try—it could have gone something like this," he said, frowning a little harder, his voice low and a bit tentative:

> *"Now I lay me down to sleep,*
> *I pray the Lord my soul to keep,*
> *And if He wants to keep it long*
> *I hope He will not think it wrong . . ."*

He hesitated here, mouthing words silently until he had the rhythm he wanted, and went on:

> *"I hope he will not think it wrong*
> *Of me to ask Him now and then*
> *To let me go and play again."*

That ready, delicate facility with words is complemented in him by a remarkable acquaintance with all kinds of things, garnered, as often as not, from unusual and unexpected sources. A friend of ours came to visit, a warmhearted, witty designer with a soft, crumpled face; he had become passionately interested in Lincoln.

"Did you know," he said with genuine excitement, "that this soldier got into terrible trouble—they were going to shoot him, I think—and his mother—can't remember her name—she'd known Lincoln when he was a boy—mended his clothes and cooked for him—and she came all the way to Washington, to the White House, to plead with him—to get the kid discharged—but the guards wouldn't let her in—"

"Hannah Armstrong," Dexter said.

"How the hell'd you know that?" Our friend was half amazed, half irritated.

Dexter laughed. "I once wrote letters for old John

Armstrong when I was a child on my grandfather's farm. He was Hannah's other son. Duff's the one you want. I was eight, and old John Armstrong—he must have been close to eighty. He was illiterate. And he was struck dumb at the thought that an eight-year-old could write letters. He said over and over to my grandfather, 'He's clever. By God, he's clever.' "

After four years, when Dexter's novel, *The Cloud Chamber,* was finished, we decided it was time to try the United States again; we sold the house, put the furniture into storage, and set out—the three of us—taking the Riley on board the *Alexander Pushkin,* flagship of the Russian line, and the first passenger ship across the ocean that spring, to visit New York.

"Well, of course, you were very close to London there, weren't you?" Marvin said. He was an old colleague of Dexter's from Consumers Union days, a lawyer and a man of wide and varied interests. "Wonderful theater in London. Some of the best music in the world."

"We didn't get up to London very often—not really."

"Pretty active social life down there in Surrey, was there?"

"I don't know," I said. "We hardly ever saw anyone."

Marvin knitted his brows. "Of course, the hunting's first rate. You do much of that, Dexter?"

Dexter shook his head. "I haven't owned a gun in thirty years."

"Golf?" said Marvin tentatively. Dexter shook his head again. "Tennis?" I shook mine. "Riding? Swimming? Chess? No? Cricket? Lawn bowls? No? But what did you *do* for four years?"

A year later, after *The Cloud Chamber* came out, we took Alexander and the Riley on the *Queen Elizabeth II* and returned, this time to Devon, to the ancient borough of Totnes, protected from invaders by the town castle and by ramparts that have stood since Saxon times. We bought a house just inside one of these ramparts; the deeds, on heavy parchment, dated back to 1783, and the inner walls, in heavy stone, went back some two hundred years before that. The front of the house was hung in Welsh slate and the high garden walls enclosed a small patio and lawn trimmed with lilac and laburnum. Champagne raspberries dominated the vegetable patch, and beyond these stood a handsome stone building big enough to provide a garage for the Riley. Above the car, in a loft where a man named Shaw-Jones had once cured mackerel, we made a study for me that looked out over sloping, sheep-filled meadows. Alexander ran off each morning to the Totnes Infants' School, just around the corner and down the hill a few yards, and came back each afternoon trailing pictures of lions and sea birds portrayed in exuberant splashes of poster paint. Dexter embarked on a new novel, and I went back to renovations and daydreams and reading.

During my first year at Columbia I had taken a course in set theory, which I'd very much enjoyed, and along with my reading I had come to play at elementary mathematics; my approaches were tentative, progress was slow, and my application at best erratic. We went abroad for long trips after we'd settled in Totnes, and I took my texts along with me to Portugal and France and Switzerland; I studied them while Alexander attended local schools, learning smatterings of one language and then of another, and while Dexter worked at his new novel, which was not moving along as smoothly as he had hoped. Bit by bit, over the course of several years, I came to understand what was involved in basic algebra, trigonometry, elementary calculus, what was once known as college algebra—my books were often out of date—the beginnings of number theory, a little pure math and some history too. And in the evenings, around French or Portuguese or Swiss fires, as well as around Devonian ones, Dexter and I discussed the difficulties I had understanding what I read and the difficulties he was having putting to paper what he had in his head.

During one such discussion I told him I had an idea he just had to use; I'd been working a little with probability, and I insisted there was a charming short story in it, a parable of sorts, making fun of statistics. We were in Switzerland at the time, in a house high in the Bernese Oberland, up above the valley in which Meiringen lies and across from the Reichenbach falls, where Sherlock Holmes fought his famous battle with Professor Moriarty. I tried and tried to explain my idea; Dexter listened and listened. In the end he shook his head. "A line, a phrase, maybe," he said, "but I don't see where the *story* is." He shook his head again. "You'll just have to write that yourself."

In Switzerland they say that if you need luck you must touch a chimney sweep; the man who serviced our boiler was tall and dour, blacked and smudged all over like chimney sweeps in fairy tales, and he carried his brushes in a quiver on his back. He held his ash-covered hand cupped like a beggar's when I paid him, but I laid the coins and the pretty Swiss ten-franc note on his palm even so and touched his wrist with the tips of my fingers; he made me a small, formal bow. I wrote my story and showed it to Dexter, then rewrote it under his tutelage. A friend of his, an agent in New York, sold the story to *Harper's* and I became, at least officially, a writer. It was only then, some fourteen years after my last class at Carnegie Hall, that the dream stopped.

I had had it the first time when I was fourteen, not long after my abortive appearance on stage in the temple scene of *Aïda,* and it consisted, doubtless predictably, of a simple recapitulation of the terrors of that night. From then on I dreamed a version of those terrors whenever I slept. The costume I wore became more and more exotic from year to year, plumes and fur and trains and crowns, trimmed often, in the way of dreams, with quotations from the books I had read or with newly learned mathematical formulae, and the words and symbols scintillated in the brilliant light that filtered backstage to where I stood trembling against the black curtains of the wings. I could never remember the part I was supposed to dance; disjointed sequences of steps floated through my head like snatches of advertising jingles, and I went on stage, goaded not by courage but by terror. The terror that met me there was more awful still, and it grew and grew until the dance—and the dream—ended in the humiliation that was its only possible end.

But with that first short story it was over. And yet still around the fire, occasionally, late of an evening, I would cry out to Dexter: "How could I have failed so miserably?"

During one damp winter in Devon, when my outbursts along this line had been rather more intense than usual, Alger Hiss, who is an old friend of Dexter's, came to spend Christmas with us. We had other guests as well that year, and Dexter took them in the Riley up over the moor to see the tors in the bleak and misty landscape. Alger, who is reedy in build, and has the elegant courtliness of a royal privy councillor, stayed behind with me; I sat opposite him peeling chestnuts into a chipped enamel bowl.

Practically from the moment judgment was pronounced against him—more than thirty years ago now—Alger began the long fight to clear his name: that Christmas he was working on his writ of *coram nobis*, a little-used appeal drawn from the ancient and Topsy-like growth known as common law; the Freedom of Information Act had given him grounds for it in allowing him to discover that the FBI had suppressed evidence in his favor. The essence of a *coram nobis* is that it is addressed to the very court which rendered the original judgment—justice to supplant injustice at the source itself—and the prospect of peeling back the present, plucking out a piece of the past, and retouching the scar right at its heart had a powerful appeal to me just then.

Alger was full of hope, but he didn't talk much about it—at least not to me with the bowl of chestnuts on my lap. He talked instead about his conversion to the Episcopal Church, about his fondness for his sister, who had taught Lady Bird Johnson to play volleyball, about the many friends who had stayed by him through his troubles, about Christmas and England and the sweet-smelling daphne outside our door, about different kinds of blackbirds and the pleasures of a good claret.

"In the final accounting, Joan," he said, smiling, "I have to say I've led a happy life."

On the BBC during that same Christmas, I heard a story about a feckless Chinese youth who had been sentenced to an indefinite term of reeducation for stealing. At first the boy claimed innocence, and kindly administrators explained that his protestations were a breach of faith with the revolution and thus in themselves a demonstration of his guilt. His sentence stretched longer and longer; over the years, with the help of the administrators, he came slowly to admit his guilt and finally to believe in it. In fact, his reeducation was so complete that he was taken onto the staff of the administration, where, as one who knew from experience, he acquired an evangelical belief in the importance of admitting guilt; he was a happy man at last, a man with a mission, and he proved superb in dealing with other offenders. And then one day the administrators, reviewing his case as though served with a Chinese writ of *coram nobis,* discovered conclusive evidence that he had, in fact, been innocent all along. When they told him so, he killed himself.

The way I saw it, that Chinese made the mistake of relying on others, and the others—as others will—betrayed him. They may not have meant to, but that's how it turned out. Alger, on the other hand, relies first of all on himself, and so betrayal, when it came, failed to destroy him. For all that's happened to him, he's filled with joy when the moon rises bright and clear over apartment blocks in Manhattan; I remember him flinging an arm around Dexter's shoulders late one evening on West End Avenue—we were still living on Riverside Drive then, and we'd talked the Vietnam War all evening—and saying, "Look at that moon, Dexter! You *have* to have faith in people on a night like this!"

And so, pondering faith in oneself and faith in humankind (and somewhat to my surprise), I started in on a novel that drew its line from the story of the Chinese man and its lesson from Alger's self-reliance. I called my book *The Impostor* when I finished it, and George Braziller published it in 1979. But in between the finishing and Braziller's purchase I went through a spell of depression, as writers occasionally do at such times. It was late summer, and I began building some retaining walls in the garden of our house in Totnes. I thought building walls might work off my depression and take some of the soft flesh on my thighs with it; I built some forty feet and ran out of stones.

I discussed these things, soft thighs and the sadness of running out of stones, with my friend Brenda, a pretty woman with animated gestures, who lives down the street.

"You were a ballerina once, weren't you?" Brenda said. I shrugged; nondancers tend to think of all dancers as ballerinas, and patient explanations of the difference between the one and the other sound to them like exercises in hair-splitting. "Well, at my Natalie's ballet school they've started a mummies' class. Natalie's signed me up for it. She says I'm fat. If you go, I'll go."

On the BBC not long ago, Beryl Grey, the English ballerina and one-time director of the London Festival Ballet, said in an interview, "You cannot, if you are a dancer, take off on a three-week holiday." She was not referring to cutthroat competition or the rigidities of theatrical management. After three weeks off, a dancer's muscles are sluggish; they ache, and the fine kinetic adjustments of balance and timing are out of tune. Thirty-two counts of a jumping exercise—the standard amount—are hard on the lungs. The tendons have tightened some and the joints have lost elasticity. Steps that had been relatively easy before are now difficult, and the flaws in them, which may have taken years to iron out originally, are not always easy to rediagnose and recorrect; injuries due to strain are a constant threat.

Furthermore, dancers, like athletes, live in a world of enforced youth; when the pressures are removed, many of them settle abruptly into a soft and indulgent, often premature, middle age. I was not yet twenty when I stopped dancing, and probably for that reason alone my weight thereafter never went much beyond the average for my height; but the average for my height is almost twenty pounds over what I weighed when I was dancing, and at thirty-seven, I was soft with indulgence myself. My thighs were large and wavy and my belly gently rounded. I still held my spine rather more upright than most people (and I still had indentations across my Achilles tendons where the toe shoe ribbons had cut for so many years). My feet were still wider and smaller than they had been when I was thirteen and just beginning at the San Francisco Ballet School; the muscles of the feet pull the bones together in dancers, and in under a year there I had gone from a 7½AAAA street shoe to a 6½B, which I still wore. And that was about all.

I bought a black leotard that was too large and black tights that were too long, and Brenda took me to a charming Georgian house at the western edge of Paignton, a little resort town on the English Channel four or five miles from where we lived. A sign in front of the house read: "Torbay School of Dancing." We entered a small, cold room furnished with purple chairs and a box bench with flowered cushions. "It tends to fall in if you sit on it," Brenda warned. From the room beyond, a piano played out heavily accented rhythms, and the old familiar smell of fresh sweat hung in the air.

There were seven mummies in all, dressed in a variety of costumes. One wore a green leotard and panty hose, another a tiny yellow skirt and T-shirt, another wore all black (she had had ballet lessons as a girl). One was barefoot. "Why ballet lessons?" said a stocky, muscular young woman in response to Brenda's question. "Well, it makes a change, doesn't it?"

A *reverence* (the final curtsy) played in the room beyond, and a number of little girls in pink tunics filed out and past, sweaty, talkative, and totally unseeing of us. A smiling face appeared around the studio door— blond hair tied back in a ponytail, blue eyes both friendly and amused, prominent teeth.

"This is Mrs. Webber," said Brenda.

The studio was no more than thirty feet by fifteen; patchy green linoleum covered a floor which I gauged to be half wood and half stone. There were low barres for small children along the sides of the room, high peaked windows at either end, and mirrors in the spaces between window and wall at the far end. At the near end at an upright piano sat a large lady who was eating chocolates from an open box beside her. She looked guilty and wiped her hands surreptiously on a napkin. "All right, ladies, first position," Mrs. Webber said, straightening her back, placing her own feet in first position by way of demonstration, and directing a stern glance at the pianist. *"Pliés, please."*

Jill Webber is a small woman with upright carriage; she is pert and pretty, with a body and a bearing much like Alice's in Tenniel's illustrations for *Alice in Wonderland*. She wore a full skirt that evening and a pair of what I came later to know as English teaching shoes; her small, strong, well-proportioned feet plainly displayed in their turn-out her years of training. I had expected an English Wanda Wenninger, and I found

Mrs. Webber all the more charming for not being one.

Getting down into that first *plié* wasn't too bad, but getting up again was a different matter; fortunately it wasn't followed by many more. There was something funny about the music; I couldn't count it. The positions were very uncomfortable. I hadn't remembered them that way. My hip joints, and my knees and ankles as well, felt twisted and constrained; my feet seemed to have grown bigger and wider.

And what I saw in the mirror genuinely puzzled me. I had expected, perhaps in deference to my age and condition, the remnants of my San Francisco training, some evidence of seemly restraint, some personal austerity. Instead my arms and hands moved in a style wholly recognizable in its New York orientation; they looked independent of me, cocksure, expressive of that peculiar freedom I had so disliked when I'd been a pupil in San Francisco watching the strawberry blonde from the New York City Ballet. They embarrassed me a little, my arms, and I wasn't sure whether I was pleased with them or not.

In the center Mrs. Webber set us a polka; I had danced a polka at a Polish wedding twenty years before. "Come now, ladies," she said, "you can do it if you try. It's perfectly simple. One, and-two. One, and-two. One, and-two."

But I couldn't seem to get the logic of it. I couldn't shift my feet about and turn at the same time, and the music seemed to bear no relation to the steps. One, and-two. I feigned irritation—I had run into the wall, anyway—and went off to one side to study the situation. Standing still, I could count the music easily; the beat was, if anything, obnoxiously clear. I tried the dance again, and again heard nothing but amorphous musical wanderings.

The class ended. I felt dissatisfied. I wasn't any more tired than I had been building walls, and I couldn't even do a polka. I handed Mrs. Webber the sixty pence that constituted her charge for the class.

"Look," I said, "do you have a class with, well, teenagers in it?"

"Monday night at a quarter to eight," she said, her voice amused, even teasing a little.

My Monday night classmates, unlike the ill-clad mummies, sported full regalia—tights, leotards, pulled-back hair, and ballet shoes or pointe shoes with the shanks removed. There were half a dozen of them, and they chatted together in the dressing room about school and diets, how their feet hurt and what to do about blisters. From time to time they glanced at me curiously, but no one of them addressed me, and I found myself appraising their legs and bodies with a largely forgotten streak of San Francisco Ballet School nastiness combined—not too comfortably—with a streak of envy for their youth. They seemed much preoccupied with some sort of dancing examination three of them were about to take. I'd never taken an examination in dancing in my life; the thought that some people might do so had never occurred to me.

The class itself wasn't difficult, but it was not like the mummies' class at all. It was a real ballet class, and by the end of the barre my whole body trembled and my head ached. In the center, only the trick of pirou-ettes stayed with me. Everything else was gone. To my surprise, I couldn't remember the names of most of the steps, and those few I could remember I could no longer execute. I did remember how my body should feel when it moved, but I couldn't make it feel that way. My legs were bags of cement; I couldn't keep my balance at all, and when I jumped I got nowhere.

After the *reverence*, I walked around the small studio pretending to inspect the walls while covertly using them to keep myself upright. Dolls in national costumes stood on shelves there, and numerous framed certificates hung near the piano. Mrs. Webber watched me with a smile, smoking a cigarette. Among other things, the framed certificates stated that Jill

Webber had passed her Intermediate and Advanced examinations and had been admitted as an Associate Member of the Royal Academy of Dancing; they looked like diplomas in a doctor's office, and they were signed by a number of people, most flamboyantly by Margot Fonteyn de Arias, who has an angular, showy hand.

"What do all these mean?" I asked.

"Don't you have ballet exams in America? No? How do you keep up standards in small towns, then?"

"We don't."

"Well," she said, taking a deep breath, "in England we have the RAD—the Royal Academy of Dancing— and any teacher who belongs to it has taken these exams. They're supposed to prove that I know what I'm doing and can teach to a set standard."

"What class is this one? The one I just took?"

"Elementary." She blew out smoke and fanned it away from my face with her hand. "You go through four basic grades, then comes pre-elementary, then elementary, then intermediate, then advanced. Come and have a coffee some afternoon. I'll tell you all about it."

The Monday night elementary class revolved around Heather and Julie and Tracy, who were preparing for this strange exam, and I watched them during the center work when I had the energy. They were obviously well-trained, but all three were at least sixteen, which I thought old for the level they had reached; they weren't without talent, though, and they said they wanted to be professional dancers.

Heather was preparing to audition for a scholarship to one of the numerous resident theatrical schools in London, and up until a few months previously her chances, according to Mrs. Webber, had been good. But Heather had broken a bone in her foot in class one night, and she wasn't long out of plaster. She was a slender girl, tall and full-breasted; the careers adviser at her school had suggested she become a policewoman. Her father was sending her brother to a private school, and there wasn't much money left over for Heather's education. The injury to her foot gave focus to some rather bitter feelings. To Mrs. Webber's exhortations to work harder, she said, "What's the use? I'm not going to pass." And to anything suggesting that she could do better if she wanted to, she shrugged and clenched her teeth. Julie, watching her from across the room, smiled faintly, much as I myself would have been only too happy to smile all those years before had Harold Christensen spoken like that to Suki. Julie had already failed the exam once, and Heather was her best friend.

Heather had to go all the way to Bristol to take her examination, and during the Monday class afterward there was a buoyancy in her manner I hadn't seen before; I decided she thought she'd passed. But she hadn't. Her exam report arrived a week later; it said she was "sitting in the hips" and that her turn-out was "weak." Heather didn't cry, but the buoyancy left her and she took to making sarcastic comments in class.

By this time all the girls knew that I had been a real dancer once; they whispered about it among themselves, and they watched me curiously in class. They danced, according to the dictates of the Royal Academy of Dancing, with an austerity not unlike the style of the Christensen brothers, and my flamboyant arms puzzled them; despite my age and poor condition, though, I was not technically inferior to any of them, and I turned much better than all of them. In the dressing room they had come to ask me the occasional deferential question about ballet in New York and to complain to me about the shortcomings they saw in the English system of training. But after her failure Heather no longer spoke to me in the dressing room, and in class I seemed to irritate her beyond bearing. "Oh, Joan," she said, "what are you trying so hard *for?*" One evening, when I managed three good double turns and ran into the wall on the fourth, she said,

"Why don't you just give up?" I was aware I worked harder on Monday nights than I had any reason to, and like Heather, I was beginning to wonder why. I was not sorry when she disappeared, taking her uncomfortable questionings with her.

Heather had gone, it turned out, to a number of auditions in London, and had finally taken a job with a cabaret troupe from Paris. A postcard appeared one day on the bulletin board in the little dressing room; it was addressed to "Dear Elementary" and it said that Paris was exciting and that being a professional dancer was fun. It was signed, "Cheers, Heather."

As for Julie, she passed her exam on her second try and Tracy passed hers on the first; both went on to ballet schools in London. I was especially sorry to see Tracy go; she had wobbled in the slow work so much worse than I that her presence had come to reassure me. On the other hand, she'd picked up combinations of steps quickly and she jumped well. The exhilaration I remembered accompanying jumps was only a faint memory; the reality was awful.

I could count the music at last, though; for a while it had remained amorphous and then one night, without warning, it was perfectly clear to me again. And I could now manage the barre, given the standard of the class, reasonably well. One of the plump ladies from the mummies' class watched elementary class one night. "You've improved ever such a lot, Joan," she said afterward. "You don't run into the walls anymore."

And Tracy, not long before she left for London, had said, "You know, Joan, when Mrs. Webber told us a lady was going to join us, I thought you'd hold us back. I said to myself, 'I bet she's going to be fat and forty.' And you're not either."

I was pleased out of all proportion by these comments.

I had begun to work once or twice a week by myself in one room of our house in Totnes, where Dexter installed a barre and a mirror wall for me. Three or four hours of that spread out over the course of seven days was enough to make me too tired to write—which at least gave me an excuse not to—and then Jill Webber set up an extra class for three of us: an ex-pupil named Tamzin Leveson; somebody's mother, who had been a dancer twenty years before; and me.

Somebody's mother was, as Tracy had feared I would be, fat and obviously past forty; she had back trouble too, and soon the class consisted only of the ex-pupil and me. Tamzin Leveson is taller than I am, close to five feet nine inches, and her complexion has the delicate luxury and blush of a white peony. She is strikingly pretty: hazel-eyed, blond, with an upright bearing and a carefree, graceful walk. There is an earnestness about her person and an aloofness too, a chaste stillness, as though she were a maiden from the days of knighthood, portrayed in tapestry, her hand resting on the unicorn's cheek. I found her difficult to talk to at first. She had passed her Elementary examination and had then auditioned for and been accepted by the Royal Academy. For three years she trained there, passing other examinations along the way, to become on graduation one of the tiny, select group of licentiates of the Royal Academy of Dancing; as such, she is one of the most highly qualified teachers of ballet in England. She is also a very accomplished dancer.

In this new class of two I strained and pulled and jerked at my body like one possessed; my muscles were sore all the time, and I reactivated an old bunion and acquired a large stone bruise and a number of minor aches and pains. The only part of the lesson I really enjoyed was the pirouette section; I had forgotten what a fine sense of physical freedom and defiance there is in spinning around on tiptoe, in control of a trick that defeats almost everybody else. I enjoyed the hardening of my muscles too, and the loosening of tendons; the flesh on my thighs was tighter, my belly flatter, and my twinges of arthritis rarely bothered me anymore. I lost fifteen pounds rather abruptly then, and the image I saw in the mirror, carefully garbed in black, took on a semblance of the figure I had once had.

And the look of my right foot, the foot with the stone bruise, quite pleased me. I had jumped down the stairs of the 116th Street subway station one night years before while I was a student at Columbia; some of the tarsals broke and others fractured, and the doctors said it was a good thing I wasn't dancing anymore. I'd be lucky, they said, if I could ever do such a thing as run. The foot ached a little during class at the Torbay School of Dancing, but it didn't actually hurt, and the scar tissue that had formed over the break gave it an outline not unlike the fine, high arch I had so envied in Suki's feet.

It irritated me that I hadn't had that foot when I was at the School of American Ballet; it was better-looking than my unbroken foot. I stared at it in the mirror, comparing past and present opportunities. I was, I told myself severely, almost forty; my hair was beginning to gray, and the idea I was entertaining was absurd. On the other hand, I did weigh only 120 pounds, and examining my face in the mirror, I thought I might pass for thirty with the aid of a little dye. I went to talk to Jill.

She laughed. "Turn your face toward the window. Now the other way. Now back again." I held my breath. "What about twenty-six?"

"Twenty-eight?"

"Easily, I should think. Why?"

"Do you think—well, I know it sounds stupid, but do you think I could ever get back into shape?"

"I don't see why not," she said, looking at me curiously. "People dance until they're forty and more. How old did you say you were? I've forgotten."

"Thirty-seven. Look, what I want to ask you is—

you're an expert in this sort of thing, aren't you?—do you think it might be possible for *me* to get back to a corps standard again?"

"Well," she said slowly, "let me put it this way. If I were you, I'd have a bash at it. So what can I do to help you?"

"Get me to jump again."

2

A class on pointe begins, as a regular class does, at the barre, where repetitive exercises give the dancer time to get used to the alien forward tilt of her body and the extra inches added to her height so that when she gets to the more complicated maneuvers expected of her in the center, she can negotiate them with the confidence born of a calm and orderly preparation.

THE BUS FROM TOTNES to Paignton and the Torbay School of Dancing takes about twenty minutes through country lanes, with views reaching out to the English Channel and back across the tors of Dartmoor. My challenge to Jill put me on this bus three times a week, every Monday, Wednesday and Saturday, barring holidays, from that fall to the following summer. Farmers were plowing their fields when I began these rides; patches of red Devon earth stood out starkly between the crooked lines of hedgerows dividing the small pastures from the even smaller fields of wheat and purple cabbages and turnips. The bus had to push its way through slush and deep pools of water on the road during the winter; by spring there were primroses in all the fields.

Going out of Totnes the other direction, you come to Dartington Hall, a private and expensive school and cultural center set up back in the 1920s with money from the Whitney fortune. Dartington has a reputation for fostering the arts; Stravinsky taught there, the Dartington String Quartet is based there, and the Jooss Ballet Company sheltered there during the war. There, I was told, a former Russian ballet dancer by the name of Kira Strakhova gave a weekly class for students at the school. The class met on Friday, which fitted well in my schedule, and the first Friday after I heard about it I arranged to meet this Russian in the faculty tearoom.

"Well, hello, Joan," she said, calling out to me as soon as I arrived. "Will you have a cup of tea? Tell me all about yourself." The open smile was as American as the accent. "Who did you study under? Doubrovska? Really? I knew her well. Years and years ago in Paris. And Vladimirov? Oh, my goodness, I took classes with him at the Salle Pleyel. And Danilova too? And Youskevitch? I knew them both. And Balanchine? Isn't that extraordinary! Why, when I first saw him all the girls were madly in love with him. I was myself. William Dollar? Him too? You didn't!" She smiled. "Now, I really did love him. He used to visit my family in Florida and take me out to shows. I loved him dearly. Even Germaine Ogier? Where'd you get to meet her?"

I asked her if she was, in fact, American.

"Oh, yes," she said. "I was born in Saint Louis, Missouri."

"How'd you get a name like Kira Strakhova in Saint Louis?"

"I didn't. I got it in Paris. My mother took me to Paris to study when I was ten, and I joined the Ballet Russe when I was fourteen. Colonel de Basil chose me—and the name too. My name was Patsy Thal. 'We can't have a name like that,' he said. 'How's Patsy Thal going to look alongside Tatiana Riabouchinska and Natalie Krassovska and Tamara Toumanova?' "

Dartington's ballet class took place in the school's gymnasium, and Kira led me through a tortuous path of dimly lit hallways, ugly battered doors and smells of disinfectant to reach it. Along the way we picked up an enormous, old-fashioned tape recorder.

"No piano?"

"You can't have a piano in a place like this," she said. "The children here—well, we had a piano to start with, but we lost keys and then we lost the whole front."

The room was very large; there were baskets for basketball at either end, and four large teenage boys bounded about, intent on a disorderly game.

"Bring your things in with you. Things tend to disappear around here. This is Liz. She runs the tape for me. Now, shoo!" she said, addressing the boys. "Shoo!" They played on. "Now look here, this is time for my class. Get out! Go! Go on!"

I dressed in an evil-smelling bathroom with mud on the floor and paint peeling off in large pieces from the walls; the toilet chain was broken, the seat missing, and an old soccer shoe floated, sole up, in the dirty reservoir of water in the bowl. Back in the gym, a few girls about fourteen years old appeared, smiling shyly and holding their hands across their naked thighs; one or two were barefoot. There was one girl about seventeen, dressed, as I was, in leotard and tights; I eyed her warily and she eyed me.

"This is Frederick," Kira said, drawing forth a blushing teenager in tight jeans and heavy boots. "He's my only boy." The class began. In front of me Frederick let himself down awkwardly into a *plié;* his boots creaked and his jeans stretched dangerously across his bottom. Kira set the exercises that followed, but few of the girls understood what she wanted of them; they tittered among themselves when her back was turned. The counter on the tape recorder didn't work, and Liz, looking harassed, played slow music for quick exercises and quick for slow. But once in the center, I decided the seventeen-year-old in leotard and tights was lousy, and I began to enjoy myself.

"Oh, Joan," Kira said after the *temps lié*, "that was lovely. Just lovely. Why, I'm going to write Balanchine. Imagine training dancers to keep their techniques like that for all those years. What a feat!"

My Dartington Fridays, I decided then and there, were very pleasant indeed; I went regularly.

One Friday, entering the gym, I saw a dancer leaning up against the climbing frame that served for a barre, a real dancer; I hadn't seen that arrogant stance—except in the mirror—for almost twenty years. She wore a filmy skirt over her leotard and tights, and when she spoke, she had a deep, lovely voice, like my mother's. "I'm Linda Goss. We're the geriatric complement of the class, I gather," she said.

Kira is protective about Linda's story. "Oh, no," she said, when I asked her to tell it to me formally. "That's Linda's story. It's not for me to be telling you that." But I had picked up some of it. I knew that at eight or nine Linda had started taking lessons at Kira's own small, provincial ballet school in the small, provincial town of Dartmouth, a dozen miles from Totnes. From the beginning Kira had seen the talent in her, but her parents didn't have enough money to send her to a professional school, and if it hadn't been for Kira's exuberance, Linda wouldn't have a story to tell.

When the Bolshoi Ballet was on tour in London many years ago, Kira went to see a rehearsal, and having seen it, decided then and there that she wanted to go to Russia to see how such dancers were trained. Nobody at the rehearsal had sufficient authority to assure her entrée to the Bolshoi Ballet School should she get to Moscow, but someone gave her the name of a London hotel and a room number. "Ask the man who answers the door," her informant said. "He might be able to help you." She did just that, and the man who answered the door turned out to be the director of the Bolshoi Ballet Company; he was only too pleased to do a small favor for a forthright, Russian-speaking American lady who had danced with the celebrated defectors from the great Maryinsky Theater in Leningrad. And the teachers at the Bolshoi Ballet School were as interested in Kira, when they met her on her trip to Moscow a few years later, as the director had been.

"Would you take a talented English girl?" she asked them more or less on impulse. "Could you?"

So Kira took Linda to Moscow to audition, and the audition was successful. Back in Dartmouth, the local paper reported the story and brought forth a local patron, who agreed to underwrite Linda's traveling expenses; at twelve years of age, Linda set off to Moscow on her own. Once there, she lived only with Russians, and she trained as only the Bolshoi Ballet School trains; she was classically educated too, as all Bolshoi pupils are, and she emerged some six years later as a graduate of the Bolshoi Teaching School. During the past ten years or so she has taught company classes for half a dozen major ballet companies in Europe; she speaks Russian like a Russian, and she knows Pushkin and Tolstoy and Chekhov in the original. "You know, Kira," Linda's mother said one day recently, "if you hadn't taught ballet to little girls in Dartmouth, Linda would probably be standing behind a counter in Woolworth's right now."

With the addition of Dartington, I had regular classes on Mondays, Wednesdays, Fridays and Saturdays. On Thursdays Jill came to Totnes to teach, and she agreed to work with me in the early afternoon before her regular pupils arrived. She rented the Seymour Hotel's ballroom, a huge, rectangular space with a highly polished floor and a wall of arched windows overlooking the river Dart, which runs by at Totnes's feet; I dressed straddling the toilet in a cubicle of the ladies' room and wet the bottoms of my ballet shoes in the toilet basin. My barre was the back of a plastic chair, and toward the end of my class, my audience comprised a dozen three-year-olds in green leotards hanging onto their mothers' skirts.

That left only Tuesdays, and so on Tuesdays I worked in front of the mirror in the small room Dexter had fixed up for me in our house in Totnes, running up and down stairs in the middle of an exercise to put water on to boil or rescue a roast from burning. Jill loaned me her official Royal Academy Elementary Examination tape, an ugly collection of tunes which I played over and over, repeating and repeating individual steps to get them right and then repeating and repeating to perfect them. My jump improved steadily, and little by little something of an all but forgotten excitement began making itself felt.

During the Christmas holidays, when neither Jill nor Kira taught, Tamzin and I took class together on our own; we alternated roles as teacher and pupil. She was interested in my American training and wanted to explore it for elements that might strengthen her own approach to teaching; I taught her sometimes as Doubrovska had taught me, sometimes as Vladimirov had, sometimes as Danilova, sometimes as Harold Christensen. And she taught me, relentlessly attacking small technical details and carefully building approaches to conquer more major ones; she is imaginative and sure of touch as a teacher, and a delight to watch as well: head held high, cheeks flushed, long elegant body in flowing circular skirt, and feet in English teaching shoes.

In January, Jill's and Kira's classes started up again; there was snow and ice on the Totnes Road; I pressed myself harder and harder, and the injuries began. One morning I strained the long slender tendon that hooks down over the ankle bone on the inside of the foot; Jill's mother, Mrs. Soundy, prescribed her physiotherapist.

"Mr. Wright's ever so good," she said. "He's the official physio for Torquay United. The football team. You see him out on the field whenever a player gets hurt. He treats Sue Barker too. She's Devon's hope for Wimbledon this year."

Mr. Wright used ultrasound, massage and heat on my ankle, and after two weeks it was no longer painful. The calf muscle on my right leg went next; it took two weeks of treatment too. Not long after that I forced myself down into a complete split at long last and pulled the huge tendon that connects the thigh to the pelvis at the back of the leg. And I landed badly one day and sprained another ankle tendon. The number of my calls on Mr. Wright began to make me feel a little foolish.

Even when the injuries themselves weren't painful, I ached all the time; my muscles were often sore to the touch, and going up and down stairs I had to grasp at the handrail. I took long, hot baths and applied mustard plasters that smelled of camphor. But there is an exhilaration in regaining control over the body, a sense of an ancient right reclaimed, that tends to overpower whatever minor indignities accompany it, whether multiple calls on a physiotherapist or a clumsy gait on the stairs, and like a body-builder with oiled skin, I posed for myself in front of mirrors, admiring me first from this direction and then from that. Dexter admired me too. And Kira. "You've got the body of a teenager," she said one day. I admired my belly, which was unrippled and flat despite a pregnancy and, ten years after giving birth, a botched abdominal operation that left me with a foot-long scar and a clutch of cut muscles. I admired my thighs, so recently the soft and gently corrugated thighs of a middle-aged lady, now firm and smooth. And I admired, too, the clean, hard lines of muscle that decorated my abdomen, my back and my calves.

But had I thought about it much, I would have said that any effect ballet classes might have on arthritic complaints could only be negative. I probably owe the sporadic inflammation of my right hip to an old ballet injury, anyway; it started hurting in New York when I was eighteen. A doctor there diagnosed it as a "cold in the joint," and it stopped bothering me when I stopped dancing; I felt it again only after I'd begun to feel twinges around the atlas vertebra at the base of my skull some fifteen years later. By the time I took my first class at the Torbay School of Dancing I had learned how to hold my head to minimize the effect of its stiffness, just as I had learned to walk somewhat stiffly to minimize the occasional pain in my hip. After six months of ballet lessons, though, the pain and stiffness in both joints was entirely gone.

But it was my eyes that really surprised me; they'd declined steadily if slowly over the years, as most people's do, and the trend was suddenly reversed. "The muscle control is excellent," the optician said when I consulted him about a new pair of glasses. My old pair had begun to cause strain. "It's really most unusually good. And your close vision is perfect too." The glasses he prescribed were a whole diopter weaker in the right lens and three-quarters of a diopter in the left. The prescription was, as a matter of fact, almost precisely what I'd worn nearly twenty years before.

Jill seemed as pleased by my physical condition as I was myself. "I never thought you'd get as strong as you are right now, Joan, to be frank."

And Kira said, "There are plenty of dancers in companies no better technically than you are right now—in fact, there are lots not so good."

It was Mr. Wright who suggested I soak my feet in potassium permanganate to harden the skin against the blisters I told him would form as soon as I tried toe shoes again; the players for Torquay United do that every year at the beginning of their training session.

I stuck my soaked feet into a pair of satin toe shoes bought in the market town of Exeter; the pain was terrible. Shocked, I took them off and found the skin underneath pinched and red. By this time Alexander had left the Infants' School long behind him; he ran each morning across the High Street instead, through the sixteenth-century Guildhall yard, to the lowering

brick building known as the Totnes Church Junior
School, and his feet had grown until they were exactly
the same size as mine. He put one foot into a pink
shoe, tentatively balanced his weight on it, then
stumbled back and shrieked, "Mummy, how can you
bear it?" I stuffed the things with lamb's wool and
wore them only a few minutes at a time, clinging to the
barre Dexter had made me and clenching my teeth.

In May the hedgerows in Devon are riotous with
buttercups, red and white clover, clouds of cow pars-
ley like six-foot-high baby's breath, and swarms of
bright red poppies. Wayfaring trees and whitebeam
bloom in the pastures. The occasional small, irregularly shaped field of mustard, planted as green manure
to be plowed under in July, glimmers bright yellow in
among the pastures, and fields of young wheat ripple
with the breeze. Between the hedgerows there are
clear views out over the pied landscape, and from the
bus between Paignton and Totnes I could see all the
way to Dartmoor, where ancient cairns stand amid
bracken, which in May pushes up new shoots from
underneath the brown, openwork fabric of the old
year's decay.

In May, Kira said, "Technically you're really pretty
good now. A bit weak, maybe. I'd put you, say—well,
above Rambert but below Royal. Those eighteen-year-
olds at Royal are strong. Good balance. But you ought
to take some professional classes somewhere. See
what you feel like with real dancers around you."

She suggested I go to France, to Cannes on the
French Riviera, where her old friend Rosella Hightower, once ballerina with the Marquis de Cuevas Ballet, runs a school. "I've sent pupils there, Joan. They
come back with good, strong techniques. And Rosella
ought to know something about European companies.
She just might be the person you need right now."

3

Of the many steps done in the center of a pointe class, *fouettés* are the most impressive; the dancer spins, springing onto the toe of one foot while whipping her other leg around for impetus, again and again; thirty-two is the usual number, but by sixteen she begins to be afraid—a sharp physical pang just beneath the ribs—that she won't have the strength or the tenacity to do them all.

CANNES HAS ONE spectacular street, the seaside Boulevarde de la Croisette, where there are palm trees and beds of brightly colored flowers and benches and kiosks that sell freshly squeezed orange juice. The Mediterranean looks blue and pure from there, and the sails of the sailboats are white and red and puffed out full in the breeze. Stretches of the beach alongside the Boulevarde where the fancy hotels cluster are divided into segments, each differentiated from its neighbor by the color of its umbrellas, candy-striped here, blue next door, yellow and green beyond. No sand is visible. Portions of legs and arms protrude from under scalloped fringes like ham hocks at a butcher's; the famous accent on youth and high society struggles hard to justify itself to the town's now mainly middle-aged, middle-class clientele, who emerge out into the sunlight of the Boulevarde each morning with their chows and Pekinese on leads, and disappear again to-

234

ward evening into the rank upon rank of high-rise holiday apartments that line the streets between the
Boulevarde and the foothills around Cannes, once a
little fishing village.

The prices are inflated and most people speak
enough English to insult a foreigner's fumblings with
French, especially an American's. I learned what
French I speak from a Breton who lives in Totnes, and
the natives of Cannes did me the honor of thinking me
English.

"You are not American," said the estate agent who
rented Dexter and me our ugly apartment in one of the
high-rises. "You speak a little French. Americans do
not speak French." The furniture was plastic and from
the ceiling hung a six-pronged chandelier with tiny,
star-embellished shades in red plastic. Our terrace
looked onto banks of terraces in the high-rise opposite
us; we didn't use it much. The ceaseless stream of
motorbikes in the street below made enough noise at
the fourth-floor level to shake glasses on the dining
table even with the doors and windows shut.

Whatever its defects, though, the apartment was
within ten minutes' walking distance of Rosella Hightower's Centre de Danse Internationale. I bought a
ticket for sixteen classes at the office just inside the
door; on the wall opposite was an advertisement for T-
shirts bearing the legend "Rosella Hightower,
Cannes." From above came the sounds of a class in
progress, Chopin cut up into regular phrases and the
regular thump of feet in a jumping exercise. The smell
of sweat hung in the hallways as it does in all dancing
schools. The walls were decorated with pictures of
Rosella Hightower: Rosella Hightower as Odette,
Rosella Hightower in *Don Quixote*, Rosella Hightower
partnered, Rosella Hightower alone. Languorous
leotarded figures draped themselves over the steps
leading up to the studio I came to know as the Grande
Salle.

The dressing room was small for such a school, and

cramped; clothes hung everywhere and there were street shoes over all the benches. Two naked figures washed themselves in an open shower that took up a quarter of the floor space; one half-dressed girl knitted while three or four others giggled and gossiped around her. I dressed as quickly as I could, stepping over and around other dressers; from one corner came the sound of muffled sobbing. I could not see the girl's face; she had it clutched behind her fingers, which glistened with tears, but her hair was blond and fluffy, rather like poor Miranda's used to be all those years ago in New York.

The Grande Salle is a beautifully proportioned room with a high ceiling and huge windows; it is airy and light. The floor is wood—in a poor state of repair at the time—and one wall is mirror. The class I took was entitled *professionale*, and in order to accommodate all who took it, portable barres had to be brought in. At one of these stood a dark-haired, dark-complexioned young man dressed all in white; around his waist he wore a black open-weave shawl. One girl sweated inside an entirely plastic overall; a number of others wore tight plastic shorts over their leotards and sweat ran down their legs in rivulets.

In the center, people clawed for front places in the groupings. I kept to the back and watched. The young man in white was a superb dancer, powerful, incisive, clean; three of the girls were very good; about six were what I thought of as accomplished; and the rest— perhaps forty of them—were dreadful. I classed myself among the accomplished ones; I wasn't strong enough, I decided, and I wasn't loose enough. I turned better than most, though, and my technique was clean in the small jumps. There were several girls—all female dancers, of whatever age, are known as "girls"— who looked older than I, but then I had gone to some trouble in that respect.

Just before I'd left Totnes, I'd consulted Kim about makeup. Kim was just going on seventeen; her mother is called Margot because she looks like Margot Fonteyn, and Kim is her only daughter, a bright-eyed girl with small features and a passion for the details of a lady's toilette. She sat me in a strong light in front of a magnifying mirror. I gasped. "Never mind," I said. "There's nothing you can do."

"Just sit still a moment," she said, peering at me from one side, then the other. "Tilt your head up. Now down. To the right. The left. It's not bad, you know," she went on. "You've got good skin and there's no sag. Light mascara, brown eyeliner—I'll show you how—very faint eye shadow, light brown, slight whitening on the nose side of each eye—here—bit of lanolin on the mouth, no lipstick. And I'll give you the name of a good hairdresser." She stood back a moment; her face was serious and her tone reflective. "It's quite good to have no sag at your age, you know. You're very old."

She helped me buy the makeup and taught me how to apply it; she took me to her hairdresser, who restored my gray hairs to light brown.

And Kira helped me invent a more recent past. She had been given a subscription to *Dance Magazine* in 1973; she found articles on the New York City Ballet in a couple of issues, and I memorized the names of dancers and ballets listed. It seemed reasonable enough that I could have danced in New York in 1973; I had, perhaps, given up to get married or to have a child or to go to college, all of which I at least had done. Or I might have had an injury of some sort. At any rate, we decided that I was getting back into shape after a few years off, and that I did not like to talk about my past much.

The *classe professionale* was usually taught by a man known as José. He was a dark-haired, dark-eyed, fine-featured man, with something of a flamenco dancer's sensual contempt in his looks and his bearing. He carried a little bamboo stick, which he held backhand like a quirt when he entered class and which he used while he taught, sometimes like a baton and sometimes like a cattle prod. He demonstrated barre exercises for us. He flicked his hair back sharply, stretched his mouth into a tense gypsy-lust smile, and pulled his pants leg up to expose one strong ankle and the bottom swell of a well-muscled calf covered in silk stocking. "Hrrr-aaaa-ssss," he used to say, drawing out the sound long and lovingly as he let himself down into a *fondu.*

José seemed to enjoy teaching; he treated it seriously and did it well, working, as I remember Harold Christensen working in San Francisco, with a sense of pattern and direction both in his corrections and in the composition of the classes he gave us. Like Harold, too, he seemed to find his pupils' seriousness funny, and his pupils in Cannes were almost as deadpan as Harold's in San Francisco had been. *"Bonne nuit,"* he used to greet us as we waited on the stairs for our morning class while the warm Mediterranean sun poured in through the windows. *"Bonne noël."* Nobody even smiled.

José's approach to technique was closer to the Christensens' than it was to the New York Russians'; there was a technical rigidity to it, a sense of cut and chop, as though each step were separated from its successor by a physical punctuation mark. I didn't like it much. But the emphasis he put on the placement of head and back—in accordance with the flamenco-like aspect of his own carriage—was quite individual. From time to time he addressed me in English, and he spoke to another girl in Italian; most of his corrections, though, were in French, and most of these were directed at one of the three pupils I classed in my mind as very good, a temperamental girl with long, elegant legs and a pretty face. From the way she stood when he spoke to her—a little nearer than is customary—I decided the relationship between them extended beyond the classroom. I rather hoped so, anyway. From that first visit to the dressing room to my last, I found the school's atmosphere hard to take; like the San Francisco Ballet School and the School of American Ballet, the Centre de Danse Internationale oozes depression.

Rosella Hightower had written me that I could "certainly have a professional class every day and a pointe class and a pas-de-deux class in June or whenever you wish." But in June the Centre de Danse prepares to undergo examinations, and all the afternoon classes are spent on perfecting variations learned during May. So in the morning after the *classe professionale,* Dexter and I shopped at the nearby Casino Supermarché, where a woman in a white apron snares for you a fish still swimming around in a tank. The bread is baked twice a day, and so are croissants and strawberry tarts; there are huge sausages and bowls of pâté from the countryside around, cooked half-langoustes lying on beds of freshly made mayonnaise, and whole aisles of local wines, fresh fruit and vegetables. We packed a picnic basket and spent the afternoons in the mountains high above the city, coming back down again at dusk to Cannes reluctantly and only when the thin mountain air had become too cool and all the wine was drunk.

There was always a flurry in the dressing room when Rosella herself taught. I'm not sure why. The first day I saw her she was dressed entirely in white: white pants with razor-sharp creases, crisp white shirt, white shoes; her hair is white too, and her face is a lean, hard, deeply lined American gothic face. She's thin and long-limbed and she moves quickly, decisively, efficiently, with no waste gestures and no trace of affection. She addressed her pupils in both English and French, but seemed unable to find the words she wanted in either language. Frustrated, she pulled at her pupils' arms, but so far as I could tell, her gestures were no more communicative than her words. Her body, though, was still very much a dancer's body, and demonstrating on her own in front of us, she showed what she wanted clearly enough; the intensity in her carried, too, a hard, unrelenting passion for the delicacy of detail she could not express in words—and we learned from her.

As for me, I loved the afternoons in the mountains and came quickly to loathe the mornings in Cannes, but I was irritated even so that the classes Rosella had promised me I could not take because of the examination preparations she had failed to warn me about. I asked one girl, a rather nice English girl completely without talent, if the Centre de Danse examinations were like the Royal Academy examinations.

"Oh, no," she said, laughing. "We get graded, that's all."

"Graded how?"

"Well," she said, "I'll get a grade of 'good.' I always get that. It's the lowest they give. Now, that girl over there—the one all in pink—she gets 'excellent' every year."

"It never changes?"

"Well, actually you have to look at it their way, I guess. If she gets less than she thinks she deserves, she mightn't come back next year. We've all been here too long."

"Don't you graduate or something after a while? Don't they help you find a job?"

She laughed again. "Oh, no," she said.

About a week later, I overheard one of the girls I thought well of as a dancer—one who seemed to me ready to work in a company—talking to Rosella after class.

"Ballet Theatre?" Rosella was saying. "I don't know where they are now." Rosella Hightower began her career at Ballet Theatre and danced there many years. "Can't you look up an address for yourself?"

There were a number of students standing around listening, and the girl shifted nervously from foot to foot. "I think they're still on Fifty-seventh Street," I said, although I didn't really know.

There was a slight pause. "Are they now?" Rosella said, turning her lean, lined face in my direction.

"But you can find the address in *Dance Magazine* or *Dance International* or any one of a number of other publications."

"Of course. You do that." She turned abruptly and started down the stairs; the girl caught at her arm. "A note from me?" Rosella sounded incredulous. "Whatever for? What possible good would a note from me do?" And on this count I was sure she was correct.

In the dressing room afterward, there was some discussion of the incident. "I don't know where to go, either," one girl said. "I don't think I have the Balanchine body. I think I'll try, maybe, San Francisco or Ballet Theatre." She thought a moment. "Or maybe I'll just come back here for another year."

The girl with the blond fluffy hair, the one who looked like Miranda, sighed and lit a cigarette, striking the match on the bottom of her toe shoe as a cowboy might on his boot. She had a soft, rosy English complexion and dark blue, almost violet-colored eyes. "What about you?" I said. I'd watched her in class; she had plainly been English-trained, and she was, I thought, not bad at all.

"I don't know. I don't know," she said. She looked very unhappy. "I don't think I can be a dancer. I just don't think I've got it in me."

"Well, maybe you should consider getting out."

"Then there'll be nothing left at all." She spoke with the cigarette clenched almost unmoving in her teeth; her eyes filled with tears, and I sat down beside her on the narrow bench. The other girls left the room in ones and twos, and the blonde with fluffy hair told me she was from Australia and had been trained there by Royal Academy teachers through her Intermediate examination. She had lived in France for several years.

"The trouble is," she said, the cigarette still immobile between her teeth and the smoke curling up over her round, pink cheeks and into her eyes, "I spend so much time lying to myself. I mean, really, I know I'm smart enough to get out of this business. What am I doing here? Why do I bother? Why am I so afraid? I'm not even sure I want to perform. So I lie to myself—or put things off, anyway—so I don't have to listen to what I'm thinking. It's no wonder I can't understand what Rosella says: I can't even understand what I think myself." Her lips moved normally, but her voice, emerging from beyond the barrier of her teeth and their captive cigarette, had a hollow, muffled sound.

"You think too much altogether," I said. "If you want to dance you should join a company."

"I don't have any experience."

"Make it up."

She rolled the cigarette from the left side of her mouth to the right and shrugged, hands on her widespread knees and elbows turned outward. "Suppose I did and suppose it worked," she said, squinting a little to protect her eyes from the smoke. "So what have I got? Years of work just to make myself eligible for the job of cog in someone else's creation. But it's worse than that. I don't even have illusions about becoming a soloist anymore. So what am I working for?" She shrugged again, this time angrily. "To stand in a line of twenty-four girls with the sole aim of being indistinguishable from any of them. Jesus, is that me? Is that what the human spirit's for? Is that all?" She laughed suddenly. "But I couldn't do it, anyway. I don't look like an experienced dancer, and I'm too old to be anything else. Much too old."

"How old are you?"

"Twenty-three."

"Why don't you just become nineteen?" I said. "You look younger than twenty-three. You could easily be nineteen."

She looked at me sadly. "It wouldn't be anything but another lie, though, would it?" she said.

"But what difference does it make? If some ballet

master is so stupid that the number twenty-three makes a perfectly good dancer useless to him, put down the number nineteen. What possible harm are you doing?"

She leaned back and smiled, stretching her lips around that savage-looking cigarette. "Nineteen," she said softly. "Nineteen. That's a nice age. I was happy at nineteen. I wasn't so afraid then. I was even happier at thirteen."

Practice for the examinations began to invade even the professional class in the mornings; I pulled my hamstring again; a dog in one of the tiny gardens below our apartment barked relentlessly; the motorbikes whined; the days got hotter. Dexter and I were drinking so much wine during our afternoon picnics that my balance was off most days, anyway, and so we decided to leave not much over a month after we'd arrived.

Back in Totnes, I took classes as I had before I'd left, with Jill and Tamzin and Kira until Dartington and the Torbay School of Dancing closed for the summer holidays. I wrote to the cultural attachés of the Belgian, French and German embassies, and I got back from each a list of active ballet companies. I sent out letters to nearly thirty of them:

> I am writing to see if it's possible for me to audition for your company. I am not an inexperienced dancer; I danced with the San Francisco Ballet under Lew Christensen and, after that, with the New York City Ballet under George Balanchine.
>
> If you need no dancers, I would appreciate hearing from you to that effect as soon as possible; if, on the other hand, you do need dancers, I will be happy to audition for you at your convenience.
>
> Very truly yours,
> Joan Brady

During August, Jill gave Tamzin and me the keys to her studio and we worked there most days for three or four hours; by the end of September I had offers of auditions from several ballet companies. The Hamburg Ballet—the company of which my old waltzing partner from San Francisco days, Kent Stowell, had become artistic director—was holding an open audition in London in October, and Claude Giraud of the Grand Ballet Classique de France sent me a form letter saying I could audition anytime after the end of September. In December there were auditions for the Berlin Opera and the Wuppertal Dance Theater.

By early October it was plain that I had improved considerably. "That," said Jill one day when she taught me, "that's really a beautiful leg. You must have worked like hell over that." I allowed as how I had, and was greatly pleased. Jill doesn't give compliments often. And Kira said, "You ought to be able to get a job in any one of a number of ballet companies, Joan."

4

At the end of a class the dancer performs a *reverence*, a deep, sweeping, formal bow, to express gratitude to those who have taught her something of importance and to show that she has found meaning in what she has learned.

THE AUDITION for the Hamburg Ballet was scheduled for six-thirty in the evening; Dexter and I went to London during the afternoon. I had not been able to sleep very well for several nights, and I felt queasy on the four-hour train ride. I'd forgotten what it was like to be so frightened, and I arrived, cold and trembling, at the Urdang studio twenty minutes early, to become one of a crowd of dancers who squeezed through the door. There were lots of people, dressed in street clothes, talking animatedly in the entrance hall; they suggested guests at a middle-management cocktail party to me, and they ignored both the dancers who struggled to get by them to the dressing rooms beyond and the dancers who could be seen limbering up in the studio beside them. I was directed down some stairs to a basement room so crowded that I had trouble bending over to take off my shoes.

"Oh, I won't get through *pliés*," said a voice behind

me. "I'm always one of the first to go. I bet you get to *frappés* at least." Then she giggled nervously. "This place is practically solid Festival Ballet. Look at them all."

"It isn't fair," said a responding voice. "I could get into the center also. I've improved ever such a lot since you last saw me."

I couldn't tell dancers from the Festival Ballet from any of the others, but I knew that Festival was on strike. Beryl Grey, the artistic director, had never been popular; it was said she hated moving corps members up to soloist rank and soloists up to principal rank. Her financial policies, as the papers reported them, were as naive as her manner was high-handed. The dancers plainly suspected her of simple jealousy; she had been a great dancer once.

I took off my clothes reluctantly, bumping first into the naked figure on my right and then into the half-dressed one on my left. The smell of sweat was already strong in the small room; the palms of my hands were moist, and I had trouble getting the hairpins into my hair.

"Did you see old Oswald up there in that group of fools?" It was a sharp voice; its owner stood well in the midst of the room. She wore a shiny blue body suit, and her hair was slicked back into a braided bun.

"No," said her companion, whom I couldn't see.

"Well, I walked up to him and I said, 'Hello, Mr. Llewellyn,' and do you know what he did? He said, 'Don't interrupt me when I'm talking.'" She gave a short laugh. "And then he said, 'What are you doing here, anyway? You've already got a job.'"

P. Oswald Llewellyn writes a folksy column for an English dance magazine; it's not a very impressive magazine, at least by American standards, and his column seemed to me a particularly silly one, but Jill had told me he was important in the dance world. He was an expert on European companies, she'd told me; he made it his business to find places in them for graduates of the big London ballet schools.

"He said, 'You're just taking work away from someone else,'" the dancer in blue went on, "and I said, 'Mr. Llewellyn, I'm on strike.'"

"You didn't!"

"The bastard can't even get the spelling of my name right in his shitty articles."

The invisible companion laughed. "He never gets my name right, either."

There was a slight pause; the dancer in blue turned so that I could see her face and her tight smile. "Well, dear," she said, "at least he doesn't mention it very often."

It took me fifteen minutes to dress, and by the time I entered the studio, it was already filled with dancers. There must have been sixty of them, male and female, in a room designed for twenty at most, and more came in every minute. Whatever their capacities, they were all young and sleekly muscled and clothed in skintight nylon; they jostled one another for space along the walls while two identical middle-aged men, potbellied and shirtsleeved, trotted back and forth setting up portable barres in the center of the room. One issued orders in a petulant voice to his fellow and to any dancer in his path; the other, scurrying to obey, said only, "Yes, Oswald. Yes, Oswald. Yes, Oswald." The crowd in the entrance hallway was visible through the row of windows that extended along one whole wall of the studio; their chatter came through the open door, and as time wore on, they turned one by one, first just to glance in at us, to point at this dancer and that one, and finally, as the pianist and the auditioner entered the room—a full hour behind schedule—to fall silent and stare.

The auditioner was a young Englishman with brown hair; I couldn't make out his face very well without my glasses. "I want to thank you for coming, and in such numbers," he said. His voice was friendly and earnest. "And to tell you in advance how sorry I am that I can't use you all. I need only five dancers, and I need them as replacements for ones I've lost, so I'm looking for a very special type of body, and since I don't want to waste your time, I'll weed out those who aren't right as quickly as I can. But please understand that if I can't use you, it isn't a comment on you as a dancer— it's only that you aren't the body type I need right now. O.K.?" He turned to the woman who had entered the studio during his speech. "Shall we start?" he said.

The woman had brown hair too, and she was English; she was older than the man, but her manner, like his, was friendly and earnest. "I know you're all nervous," she said, while the man found himself a chair to stand on; the room by this time held well over a hundred dancers, one every eighteen inches along the barre and one every eighteen inches along both sides of the three portable barres set up in the center floor. He needed at least two feet of extra height to see out over us all. "But don't worry too much," she said. "I'm not going to give you anything very difficult." She set the first exercise, the *pliés*, motioned to the pianist, and the audition began; the air was hot and wet and full of fear.

There is a sameness about dancers at the barre, almost a uniform of physique—sleek, streamlined, nearly aquatic—that overcomes whatever disparities of decoration and style might otherwise set them off from each other; they move through ballet's elaborate and mannered paces en masse, lined up rank upon rank, mirrored back on themselves, as though they were a single body made manifold by some strange optical illusion. The *pliés* that evening included a *port de bras*, ballet's equivalent of toe-touching, but we were packed in so tightly that there wasn't room to bend over in alignment; as the dancer in front of me twisted outward to avoid hitting the rump of the dancer in front of her, I twisted outward too, and the dancer behind me did the same, and the dancer behind her. All around the room the same graceful outward movement disturbed the orderly progress of the *port de bras* like a gust of wind in a wheat field.

It is usual to begin weeding out undesirables after the *pliés,* especially when there are so many dancers present, but the man stood steadfastly on his chair while the teacher set the *tendus battements.* I was standing beside the windows into the hallway and so beside the swarm of faces that peered in at us; beyond the glass a woman in a green hat turned her eyes on me, tilted her head a little and whispered something to her companion, a small bald man with protuberant ears, who turned his face in my direction too; I stared back at them both, but their eyes, fixed on me, showed no awareness of my expression. After the *tendus battements,* in which we had to twist first inward and then outward, the teacher set the *ronds de jambe à terre,* which no twist could make possible under such conditions; yet the man kept to his chair and weeded out no one. At the end of the exercise, when it is customary to hold position, arms *bras bas,* feet in fifth, chin high, eyes out into the center of the room, I sagged back on the barre angrily instead and found to my surprise that my fear was completely gone. The faces in the window, I noticed, had lost interest in me; the teacher began to set the *frappés;* the man in charge stared out over his sea of dancers as before. When the music started, I picked up my bag from the floor beside me and walked quietly out of the room.

"But why, Joan? Why?" Tamzin sounded more puzzled than upset over the phone. "Jill said you had a good chance. You just threw it away." I told her how crowded the room was, how hot, how late the audition began. "I think I understand," she said at last. "I've known one or two girls who walked out before." She paused a moment and then went on gently. "They never seemed quite able to say why, either. But you can't let this stop you, you know."

"Auditions are no place to go all sensitive, Joan," Jill said. "Either you're a professional or you're not. And you're never going to feel right—inside yourself—until you do it. You must know that."

And so a month later I went to Paris.

The letter I'd received from Productions Claude Giraud said I should telephone ahead for an audition appointment; Kira called for me. Her French is wholly fluent. She wrote down the date and the hour, six o'clock, and the address, Salle Pleyel, 252 Faubourg Saint-Honoré, Paris. "You could have called yourself, Joan," she said. "The man I talked to speaks English." Then she laughed. "At least, he thinks he does."

Dexter and I arrived in Paris on the morning of my promised audition; we had lunch with a man Dexter had known many years before. He was frail and entirely bald; even his eyelids were bald, and his eyebrows too. He loved France, he told us simply, and because he was rich, he had come to die there. The restaurant he took us to was famous for its food and wine. But I was too nervous to eat, and I didn't dare drink. I refused when our host began to pour out the claret; I watched him taste it, rolling it around in his mouth, and I watched the two men drink it. Our host asked what we planned to do that afternoon; I told him I was due at the Salle Pleyel at six o'clock.

"Really?" he said, leaning back in his chair. "I went there on my very first trip to Paris. I was political then—very passionate—I can't for the life of me remember why. But I went to the Salle Pleyel to hear Malraux speak about China to the French intellectuals. It was a great occasion. De Gaulle was there." He picked up his wineglass as though to toast me and raised his voice. " 'You, here present, are the first generation of mankind to inherit the world in its entirety.'

That's what Malraux said. Imagine it. What a heavy responsibility! What exhilaration! The world in its entirety. Whoever'd had that before?" And then he smiled. "What kind of an audition is it?"

I told him. He put down his glass and peered at me from under his bald eyelids. "Ballet? Really? But you own the whole world, my dear. Good God, it's your birthright. With all that, you choose to make yourself into a mindless precision instrument? Why?"

I laughed and said I might well fail the audition.

"Oh, well," he said, plainly losing interest, "we all fail sometimes."

At twenty to six I made my way to the fifth floor of the Salle Pleyel, leaving Dexter at a small sidewalk café nearby. I was afraid. And I was upset, too, by what Dexter's friend had said. A pretty young man behind a desk looked me up and down, and somewhat timidly, I began the set speech I'd prepared in French for the occasion.

"All right," he interrupted almost immediately. "We speak English."

"*Je ne parle pas aussi mal comme ça,*" I said irritably, my fear giving way abruptly to vanity; I have always considered my accent pretty good. "*Essayons tous les deux.*" To my further irritation, it turned out he hadn't understood Kira after all; dancers took the *classe professionale* under Madame Daydé by way of audition, he said, and there was no *classe professionale* that evening. He did not know how he could have given Kira the impression he had. "Look," I said, half in French, half in English, stumbling clumsily between the two. "I've come all the way to France for no better reason than that your English is as lousy as my French. You made the mistake. You fix it." Worried, he suggested I speak to Madame Daydé herself; she was teaching, he said, on the third floor, and her class finished at six.

Liane Daydé is the artistic director of the Grand Ballet Classique, which serves as a showcase for her;

at eighteen she was an *étoile* of the Paris Opéra, the youngest for many generations. I have some pictures of her taken in *Blanche-Neige* in the early 1950s; they show a pretty, round-cheeked girl with dark hair in a high bun, posing beautifully costumed amid the gaudy grandeur of the Paris Opéra. The studio downstairs in the Salle Pleyel was hidden behind a jerry-built wall; my irritation at the young man had increased as I'd walked down the large, barren staircase that wound around the open grillwork of an elevator shaft, and it increased further as I waited in the cramped anteroom, pacing back and forth over the worn carpet and under a naked light bulb hanging from a wire. I could hear a class in progress. Plainly little girls. A number of teenagers passed me, eyed me curiously, and went into the dressing room beyond. They had fat on their thighs; they held their knees together; their bodies were soft and curved at the spine. I decided they were adult beginners, and for some reason the sight of them made me more irritable still. It wasn't until afterward that I realized my irritation had almost entirely overcome my fear.

At ten past six, a dozen little girls filed out of the studio and I went in. Madame Daydé is a tiny woman with dark hair, entirely recognizable as the Liane Daydé of my old ballet books. Her face, still full-cheeked, has a decidedly merry look, and a kind of innocent eagerness too; unlike the pretty young man, she listened to my prepared speech until I'd finished. Then she said in English, "But is no *classe professionale* tonight. Why you not come at ten tomorrow morning?"

Her voice was friendly and interested and her manner was open, but I found myself suddenly angry instead of irritable. Enough is enough. I'd missed out on the pleasures of my first lunch in Paris on her account and found myself an object of contempt as well; I'd be damned if worry about an audition the following day was going to ruin the pleasures of my first evening too.

"I'll be on the train back to England tomorrow at ten," I said stiffly.

She smiled. "All right, John"—she pronounced my name almost precisely as Madame Doubrovska had pronounced it many years ago—"I look you tonight."

I dressed hurriedly, breaking a supporting elastic in my leotard so that my bra showed. The soft beginners had already struggled their way through *pliés* by the time I entered the studio, but no *tendus* followed, no *ronds de jambe,* either, nor any other standard exercise; mainly we did stretches, and from time to time throughout them the pretty blonde next to me moaned under her breath, one leg stuck up on the barre as though trussed there like a chicken wing. How the hell, I asked myself, growing angrier, was I supposed to warm up with such a stupid set of exercises? But Madame Daydé paid little attention to me during them. In the center, she said, "Those is pointe shoes, John? Yes? Good. Is legs warm?"

I said they were, although I didn't have the slightest idea; I was by that time so angry I could hardly feel them. The center work, unlike the barre work, followed more or less a standard class pattern. She set exercises for her beginners, an adagio, some pirouettes, some small jumps; in between these she set some at a professional level—an adagio too, some pirouettes in place, some in a circle, some *brisés*—for me to perform on my own while the others watched. I could not tell whether I pleased her or not, although once when I had performed an exercise without difficulty, she made it harder and smiled when I managed that version without trouble, either. Then she said, "Now, John, is big *enchaînement.*"

The combination of steps she proceeded to set was long and complicated, involving *grandes jetés* and *cabrioles;* it was more like a small stage solo than an exercise, and it seemed to me a handsome if taxing thing. It was not considerate, I thought, to set a thing like that for someone who should by all rights be

scared half to death. The soft teenagers lounged back
on the barre and smiled when they heard her set the
two double *piqué* turns, one right after the other, at the
end of the combination; those, they were certain, I
could not perform. The music for the class came from
a tape recorder, which Madame Daydé held in her left
arm as she taught, counting out the beat by raising and
lowering her right arm, like a referee at a knockout,
and smiling happily. I threw myself into the exercise
with a new surge of anger, got through it far more
easily than I could have hoped, and managed the double *piqué* turns at the end with a dash that on any other
occasion would have delighted me.

Each of the girls, smiling no more, kissed Madame
Daydé in turn, and then she spoke to me again, in
French. What she said had as much the quality of a set
speech as my opening to her had had; she seemed to be
telling me something about her company's financial
difficulties, but I wasn't sure. I thought perhaps she
was letting me down easily. "Am I all right for you?" I
said, interrupting her much as the young man had interrupted me an hour before. "Am I the sort of dancer
you want?"

"Yes, yes. Is O.K., John. Is O.K. Yes," she said, as
though puzzled by my question. "What English company dance you now, John? No company? Why? Ah,
you make holidays. What age, John? *Vingt-huit?*
Good. Fine." She turned to a girl who lingered by the
door. "Go get fiche for John," she said. The girl looked
puzzled, and Madame Daydé repeated the command
in French. "You fill out fiche, John. In England. In
home. Then send me." Then she laughed. "I understand English better than I speak. Like French for
you? Yes?" I nodded, and she continued in French,
speaking more slowly. The company had not yet se-
cured its state grant for the projected season. She
wasn't sure just when rehearsals would start. She
would be in touch. Did I have a place I could stay in
Paris? I took the fiche from the girl; it was an informal

document, mimeographed, on which I was to enter my name, birth date, passport number, address, telephone number. Madame Daydé shook hands with me, thanked me for auditioning, and said she hoped she would be seeing me soon.

Out on the street again, I ran to the café to find Dexter. "Meet the newest member of the Grand Ballet Classique de France," I said, hardly able to get the words out. "Or de Paris. Or something. Anyhow, I made it."

"I knew you would. How shall we celebrate?"

"What would a Frenchman do? I think I like France after all."

We left that café and found another, where Dexter ordered *pastis* for us; we drank it and walked along the Paris streets until we came to another café. We ordered vermouth cassis there, and I chattered at him, describing Madame Daydé and the soft teenagers and the tatty studio. Dexter's hair is white now, but his face shows the same uneasy amalgam of tenseness and buoyancy it has always shown, and that evening it showed unalloyed pleasure, too, at my pleasure; it delighted me just to look at him, and at the next café we ordered a split of champagne, and at the next, two glasses of Armagnac. Still I chattered at him, giggling some by then, congratulating myself and demanding congratulations, which he delivered again and again. Between cafés he steered me through the darkened streets, laughing happily sometimes with me, sometimes at me. We passed a wall of billboards and he stopped suddenly.

"There you are," he said, pointing at a tattered advertisement for a ballet company, the Paris Opéra or the Royal or the Stuttgart Ballet. An exiting line of the corps from *Swan Lake*, backs to the audience, heads bowed, arms extended out in front of them, began at the left side of the bill and disappeared diagonally off it into the distance at the right like ties on a Kansas train track.

I laughed. "Which one?"

He bent closer. "Why, that one, of course."

"But they all look exactly the same."

"Not to me," he said. "I could tell you anywhere."

He wore a long overcoat—too long; nobody wears coats like that these days—and he stood there beside me as though he weren't entirely comfortable and could never be made so. I looked at him for a moment and then at that long line of identical swans. Beyond him and the swans as well, beyond the end of this side street, I could see the beginning of the vast expanse of the Place de la Concorde, where floodlights shone against the darkness of the November sky. We walked toward it, and as we walked I took the fiche that Liane Daydé had given me out of my pocket, tore it in two, crumpled the pieces into a little ball, and we tossed it back and forth as we went on along the street, running now, until it fell.